There's no business like show business!

In 1912, long before Hollywood had a foothold in the world of movies, Flying A Studios opened its doors in downtown Santa Barbara. As one of the earliest studios on the West Coast, Flying A Studios produced more than 1,000 films, which put Santa Barbara on the map as a prominent center for movie magic.

The movie business evolved quickly. A decade later Hollywood had become the new center of international film production, but Santa Barbara never lost its celebrity allure. Since those early days, the area has continued to attract a wide range of celebrities seeking respite from the demands of Tinseltown, a mere 90 miles away.

The quiet streets and uncrowded beaches of Montecito, Carpinteria, Hope Ranch, and Summerland have always attracted internationally famous movie, television, and music superstars, who give Santa Barbara a connection to Hollywood like no other place in the world.

This book celebrates the Santa Barbara-Hollywood relationship, paying homage to some of the show business personalities from Charlie Chaplin (builder of the landmark Montecito Inn) to Jeff Bridges to Oprah Winfrey, who continue to make our town the place "where Hollywood hides"...

AMERICAN · FILM · COMPANY
INCORPORATED

· SANTA · BARBARA · STUDIOS ·

Where HOLLYWOOD HIDES
Santa Barbara

ROBERT L. McCULLOUGH
SUZANNE HERRERA-McCULLOUGH

Silent film star Mary Miles Minter with
Flying A Studios Director William Dowlan and crew, c. 1916
Courtesy of Santa Barbara Historical Museum

Robert McCullough
Suzanne Herrera-McCullough

This is a Butterfly Beach Media Book.
First Edition: October 2014.

Where Hollywood Hides ®
© 2014 Butterfly Beach Media LLC
1187 Coast Village Rd, Suite 512
Santa Barbara, Calif. 93108

www.WhereHollywoodHides.com

McCullough, Robert L., 1945-
   Where Hollywood hides : Santa Barbara / Robert L. McCullough &
Suzanne Herrera McCullough.—First edition.
   p. cm.
   ISBN 978-0-9960522-3-8

1. Celebrities—California—Santa Barbara—Homes and haunts. 2.
Celebrities—California—Santa Barbara—Anecdotes. I. Herrera-
McCullough, Suzanne.

II. Title.
CT105.M33 2014   920.0794'91
                         QBI14-600092

All rights reserved.

No part of this publication may be reproduced or transmitted
in any form or by any means, electronic or mechanical,
including photocopying, recording, or information storage
and retrieval system, without permission in writing from the publisher.

ISBN 978-0-9960522-3-8

Cover & Book Design:
Wordzworth Ltd, United Kingdom

Printed in United States of America

Contents

Dedication	1
Preface	2
Santa Barbara & Hollywood The Historical Connection	4
Dame Judith Anderson *"Lady Macbeth"*	8
Jennifer Aniston *"Rachel Green"*	11
Ross Bagdasarian, Jr. & Janice Karman *"The Chipmunks"*	12
Rona Barrett *"Miss Rona"*	15
Drew Barrymore *"Gertie"*	16
Jeff Bridges *"The Dude"*	19
Jackson Browne *"Running on Empty"*	20
Carol Burnett *"Miss Hannigan"*	23
Charlie Chaplin *"The Little Tramp"*	24
Julia Child *"The French Chef"*	27
John Cleese *"Monty Python"*	28
Kevin Costner *"Elliott Ness"*	31
David Crosby *"Turn! Turn! Turn"*	32
Tom Cruise *"Maverick"*	35
Doug Davidson *"Detective Paul Williams"*	36
Geena Davis *"Thelma"*	39
Ellen DeGeneres *"Comedy Queen"*	40
Bo Derek *"10"*	43
Kirk Douglas *"Spartacus"*	44
Michael Douglas *"Gordon Gecko"*	47
Anthony Edwards *"Gooch"*	48
Danny Elfman *"Oingo Boingo"*	51
Mel Ferrer *"Phillip Erickson"*	52
Jane Fonda *"Cat Ballou"*	55
John Forsythe *"Blake Carrington"*	56
Anne Francis *"Honey West"*	59
Dennis Franz *"Andy Sipowicz"*	60

Whoopi Goldberg *"Oda Mae Brown"*	65
Martin Gore *"Depeche Mode"*	66
Lena Horne *"Glinda the Good"*	69
Tab Hunter *"Joe Hardy"*	70
Kathy Ireland *"Cover Girl"*	73
Michael Jackson *"Thiller"*	74
Bruce Johnston *"The Beach Boys"*	77
Michael Keaton *"Batman"*	78
Cheryl Ladd *"Kris Munroe"*	81
Christopher Lloyd *"Doc Brown"*	82
Kenny Loggins *"Footloose"*	85
Julia Louis-Dreyfus *"Elaine"*	86
Rob Lowe *"Sam Seaborn"*	89
Karl Malden *"Lt. Mike Stone"*	90
Steve Martin *"A wild and crazy guy"*	93
Dennis Miller *"King of the Rant"*	94
Robert Mitchum *"Philip Marlowe"*	97
Peter Noone *"Herman's Hermits"*	98
Fess Parker *"Daniel Boone"*	101
Katy Perry *"California Gurl"*	102
Brad Pitt *"Mr. Smith"*	105
Ronald Reagan *"The Gipper"*	106
Alan Thicke *"Jason Seaver"*	109
John Travolta *"Vinnie Barbarino"*	110
Oprah Winfrey *"Sophia"*	113
Jonathan Winters *"Maude Frickert"*	114
The Santa Barbara International Film Festival	117
Roger Durling	118
Recent Santa Barbara Productions	120
Photo Credits	122

The Flying A Studios roster:
all major stars of their day, c. 1912
Courtesy Santa Barbara Historical Museum

American Film Mfg. Co. promo sheet
Courtesy Santa Barbara Historical Museum

This Book is Dedicated to...

Our careers in show business began with Suzanne breaking in as an actress at Universal, Warner Bros., and Paramount Studios, while Bob worked his way up writing and producing television shows and pitching screenplays throughout Hollywood.

Both of us are Los Angeles natives, and it wasn't until we spent part of our honeymoon in Santa Barbara that we gave any thought to the possibility of living outside of L.A.

Those thoughts surfaced when we were invited to actor Mel Ferrer's Carpinteria ranch for lunch. (At the time, Bob was working with Mel on *Falcon Crest*, the hit CBS television series.)

Mel's home was an authentic adobe hacienda overlooking the Pacific, with breathtaking views up to Gaviota on the north and down the coastline to Santa Monica on the south.

It was a heavenly afternoon, with an amazing meal and an impressive celebrity guest list.

When we told Mel we were thinking of buying a weekend place, he insisted that we meet with his real estate broker. Only two weeks later, we realized there was no better place than Santa Barbara. We soon had our "weekend" place...and it wasn't long before those weekends stretched into full weeks...and we soon knew where home truly was.

If it weren't for Mel, we would have never known the true magic of Santa Barbara. We owe him our gratitude and forever treasure our time with him, for he truly showed us "where Hollywood hides."

Preface

Santa Barbara…it's just ninety miles north of L.A.'s "entertainment capital of the world"…yet it can feel like it's a thousand miles away.

For us, it all began with a honeymoon road trip that started at the Four Seasons Biltmore, a Mediterranean-Spanish Colonial masterpiece on twenty acres at Butterfly Beach.

After traveling to San Francisco and Lake Tahoe, we headed back to Santa Barbara for a weekend in Montecito at the San Ysidro Ranch—where a veritable "who's who" of Hollywood icons including Gloria Swanson, Natalie Wood, Bing Crosby, and Jean Harlow once vacationed in privacy, away from the prying eyes of the media.

We soon learned that we were not the first honeymooners to stroll the gardens at the San Ysidro Ranch, as we followed in the footsteps of newlyweds Jack and Jackie Kennedy, Sir Laurence Olivier and Vivien Leigh, Gwyneth Paltrow and Chris Martin, and Julia Roberts and Danny Moder.

The attractions of Santa Barbara and the foothills of Montecito, the quiet streets and the uncrowded beaches, were simply too hard to resist. What better place to escape from the hectic world of power lunches, business dinners, and the obligatory weekend party circuit?

Four Seasons Biltmore Hotel at Butterfly Beach

And so—in the midstream of busy film and television careers—we found ourselves living in Santa Barbara, raising a family, and working just as efficiently as ever on all of our studio projects.

In the early 1980s, however, every agent, producer, and studio executive told us that moving to Santa Barbara would put us "out of the business." But as technology gained a foothold in the Hollywood production community with fax machines, phone modems (remember those?), email and the internet, we found ourselves entertaining showbiz friends on their weekend visits…friends who invariably began asking, "So who's your real estate agent?"

The San Ysidro Ranch in the Montecito foothills

While it has always had something of a Hollywood connection, Santa Barbara today is truly a bedroom community for the entertainment industry. Over the years we've met many wonderful people and their lovely families—some in the entertainment business and some not—and we all have one thing in common: a sincere appreciation for the good fortune to be living in such a beautiful place.

So while Santa Barbara has long been a playground for Hollywood celebrities, for many this is simply where we call home. A place of respite, a personal retreat, a world where the most valued thing we have is increasingly difficult to find: privacy.

This is the town where Oprah Winfrey walks the beach and nobody looks twice, where Kevin Costner goes out to dinner and gets the same table you had last night, where nobody asks Steve Martin for his autograph, and where Dennis Miller could easily chat you up at the local coffee shop.

Santa Barbara, including the communities of Montecito, Summerland, Hope Ranch, Carpinteria, Santa Ynez, and Los Olivos, is our home and theirs…so be assured that this book is in no way meant to disturb the sanctity of "home."

This book—while not intended to be a complete roster of Santa Barbara's show business luminaries—is simply a tribute and a "thank you" to all those celebrities who have helped to make this a very special place.

WHERE HOLLYWOOD HIDES

Santa Barbara & Hollywood
The Historical Connection

Flying A Studios – Mission at State St.
Courtesy Santa Barbara Historical Museum

In 1912, the American Film Manufacturing Company, originally based in Chicago, migrated to Santa Barbara and found the perfect mix of virgin scenery, ocean vistas, and urban backdrops around which writers, directors, and producers could create a wide range of stories.

Francelia Billington,
c. 1917

Courtesy Santa Barbara Historical Museum

Flying A Studios leading man
William H. Stowell, c. 1913-1916

Courtesy Santa Barbara Historical Museum

WHERE HOLLYWOOD HIDES

With their "Flying A" logo, Santa Barbara's earliest motion picture studios were built on an abandoned ostrich farm just north of what is now a bustling downtown commercial center. Blessed with an abundance of available labor, predictable Mediterranean climate, and breathtaking scenery, Santa Barbara soon became the gravitational center of the movie world.

Flying A Studios—with stars like Lon Chaney, Mary Miles Minter, and Victor Fleming—produced more than 1,200 films in Santa Barbara.

By the time Cecil B. DeMille went on location at the sand dunes in Guadalupe just north of the city to shoot *The Ten Commandments*, Santa Barbara's identification with Hollywood was well-established.

Between 1912 and 1917, Flying A Studios was a dominant film center, rivaled by only a handful of Hollywood upstarts. A huge studio complex had been erected at the intersection of Mission and State streets, complete with stages, horse stables, dressing rooms, and elegant office facilities. At its zenith, Flying A was one of the best equipped and most prolific film studios in the world.

Flying A Studios' leading female star Mary Miles Minter,
c. 1916-1919

Courtesy Santa Barbara Historical Museum

But failure to anticipate the changing demands of an increasingly sophisticated film audience would ultimately destroy the competitive potential of Flying A. Serious distribution problems and competition from films of greater length coming out of Hollywood would prove insurmountable.

With the impact of World War I, the Depression of 1921, a devastating 1925 earthquake, and innovative competition from Hollywood, the halcyon days of Flying A Studios came abruptly to an end.

As far as major film producers were concerned, Santa Barbara had fallen off the map. Things stayed that way for decades, but in recent years California's Central Coast—and Santa Barbara County in particular—has once again become a favorite location choice for Hollywood's filmmakers and celebrities.

WHERE HOLLYWOOD HIDES

"WHY LIVE ANYWHERE ELSE?"

Julia Child

DAME JUDITH ANDERSON

"There is nothing enduring in life for a woman except what she builds in a man's heart."

One of Santa Barbara's most esteemed and distinguished citizens—always an active and enthusiastic ambassador for the city—was Dame Judith Anderson.

Anderson first came to Santa Barbara to appear on stage in *Strange Interlude*, and discovered the allure of life on the "Gold Coast." She returned to Santa Barbara's Lobero Theatre for Eugene O'Neill's *Mourning Becomes Electra*, and forty years later played the title role of *Hamlet* on the same stage.

Anderson was one of the most highly regarded thespians of her generation, starring in theater classics such as *The Mask and the Face*, *Hamlet* (opposite John Gielgud), *Macbeth* (with Laurence Olivier), and winning a Tony Award for her title role in *Medea*.

While she expressly preferred the life of the stage, Hollywood opened its doors to her and she reciprocated with powerful performances in Alfred Hitchcock's *Rebecca*, *Lady Scarface*, *King's Row*, *Diary of a Chambermaid*, *And Then There Were None*, *Laura*, and *All Through the Night*.

Anderson was married to a theatrical producer and rancher from Carpinteria, and their ranch in the avocado groves and foothills became her anchorage to Santa Barbara.

As the Golden Age of Television came into America's homes, Anderson dignified the new medium, bringing her interpretive character work to *The Motorola Television Hour*, *Producers' Showcase*, *Climax Mystery Theater*, and *Playhouse 90*. Anderson even diverged from her classic roots, playing character roles in everything from *Cinderfella* to *Star Trek*. Perhaps as a tip of the hat to her chosen hometown, Anderson appeared as Minx Lockridge in no fewer than forty-nine episodes of *Santa Barbara*, the internationally distributed TV soap opera featuring the tumultuous life of the stunningly wealthy (and purely fictitious) Capwell family.

Anderson was a valuable Santa Barbara cultural icon and spokeswoman, often found raising money to renovate the Lobero Theatre, hosting fundraisers for the local Ensemble Theatre Company, or giving library readings for local children's groups.

Dame Judith Anderson defined an era and was truly a cultural magnet, drawing the world of arts and entertainment to Santa Barbara. Stop by the Lobero Theatre where her portrait hangs and you'll feel the presence of true star power.

Not many actors can easily make the transition from television to feature films and then to superstardom with any lasting success...but then, there is only one Jennifer Aniston!

Jennifer has been a regular on the Santa Barbara scene, making frequent appearances at the Santa Barbara International Film Festival, shopping on State Street, and enjoying personal downtime poolside at the Four Seasons Biltmore Hotel.

A graduate of Manhattan's Fiorello H. LaGuardia High School of Music & Art, Aniston appeared in a number of TV roles on shows like *Ferris Bueller*, *The Edge*, *Muddling Through*, *Quantum Leap*, *Herman's Head*, and *Burke's Law*. With her career idling along like that of so many others, she actually considered giving up the life of a struggling actress and moving on to other things.

But when Jennifer was cast in *Friends*, the part of Rachel Green made her one of the most highly paid television actresses of her generation, earning her Emmys, Golden Globes, Screen Actors Guild Awards, and American Comedy Awards.

By the time *Friends* completed its phenomenal decade-long run, Jennifer had established herself as a serious Hollywood contender as she moved into feature films with critically acclaimed performances in *Rock Star*, *The Good Girl*, *Bruce Almighty*, *Along Came Polly*, *The Break-Up*, *Marley & Me*, *He's Just Not That Into You*, *Love Happens*, *The Bounty Hunter*, *Just Go with It*, *The Switch*... and many more.

With her Hollywood status and a place on the *Forbes* magazine list of "Ten Richest Women in Entertainment," Aniston's clout is right up there with Oprah Winfrey, Madonna, Celine Dion, and Jennifer Lopez, as one of the top-selling "faces" in the industry.

It comes as no surprise that when Jennifer Aniston needs that quick weekend getaway to escape the clamor of Hollywood paparazzi, she often retreats to the anonymity of civilian life here in Santa Barbara.

JENNIFER ANISTON

"Friends"

ROSS BAGDASARIAN, JR. & JANICE KARMAN

THE CHIPMUNKS

"Keeping his father's legacy alive"

In 1958, novelty-song producer and sound engineer Ross Bagdasarian, Sr. took the technique of accelerated audio playback used in his hit record "The Witch Doctor" to new heights when he came up with a trio of singing critters known as The Chipmunks.

The lovable (and always mischievous) Alvin, Simon, and Theodore were unlikely, animated pop icons, but Bagdasarian found himself earning multiple Grammy Awards with them. Then, with Bagdasarian's untimely death in 1972, The Chipmunks quickly fell into Trivial Pursuit obscurity.

But his son Ross Bagdasarian, Jr. knew in his heart that his father's legacy could not simply be ignored. Passionate about the characters his father had produced, Ross Jr. created a series of new Chipmunk recordings and televised animated specials, all with a contemporary, upbeat twist. *Chipmunk Punk* was quickly followed by *Chipmunk Christmas*, and *Alvin and the Chipmunks* for NBC-TV. Not long afterward, Ross Jr. released *The Chipmunk Adventure* as a highly successful feature film.

The younger Bagdasarian and his business partner/wife Janice Karman are not simply showbiz deal-makers who leave the creative work to others. Both husband and wife "play" their animated characters, speaking and singing all of the Chipmunks' dialogue and song tracks, which gives Alvin, Simon, Theodore, and all the "Chipettes" their unique blend of energetic humor.

The Chipmunks are one of the most successful music groups of all time, earning five Grammy awards, an American Music Award, a Golden Reel Award, two Kids' Choice Awards, and they've been nominated for three Emmys as they continue to climb to new heights.

WHERE HOLLYWOOD HIDES

Journalist, gossip columnist, television anchor, novelist, sports commentator, and most recently Santa Barbara-area rancher, Rona Barrett is an entertainment industry innovator and self-branding entrepreneur without parallel.

Initially getting her start as a celebrity reporter with national news syndicates, Rona became a "Hollywood gossip" insider in the tradition of Hedda Hopper and Louella Parsons, appearing on ABC network affiliates nationwide. She's credited with creating the now familiar celebrity special, and establishing the format used by Barbara Walters for so many years.

Her autobiography *Miss Rona* was a best-selling tell-all autobiography that dared to identify prominent Hollywood celebrities in somewhat compromising positions. Her television work transitioned to a prolific writing career with *How You Can Look Rich and Achieve Sexual Ecstasy* and *The Man Who Will Be King: Unauthorized Biography of Prince Charles*.

Rona discovered Santa Barbara and Santa Ynez in the early 1980s. At the time, she was co-hosting NBC's very-late-night show *Tomorrow*, and was working as an unlikely sportscaster for World Wrestling Federation's WrestleMania VI. The sight of the petite Miss Rona in her usual red-carpet fashion interviewing the likes of Jesse "The Body" Ventura, Randy Savage, and Gorilla Monsoon will never be forgotten for its high-camp pure entertainment value.

Barrett reinvented herself yet again with the founding of the Rona Barrett Lavender Company, producing a wide array of products serving the bath, beauty, food, and aromatherapy markets.

A visit to her website reveals that this high-energy show business legend has transcended the world of Hollywood gossip and is now committed to supporting Santa Barbara's Friendship Center and a host of other nonprofit organizations serving the senior community.

Well beyond her Hollywood origins, Rona Barrett now enjoys the paradise of her Santa Ynez lavender ranch as she builds yet another career for herself: humanitarian.

RONA BARRETT

"Queen of Gossip"

DREW BARRYMORE

From child actor to Hollywood's "A list"

Actress, director, writer, model, entrepreneur...there isn't much this namesake and descendant of the famed theatrical Barrymore family hasn't yet achieved. The granddaughter of cinema legend John Barrymore and the great-niece of Ethel and Lionel Barrymore, if anyone has thespian DNA, it's Drew Barrymore.

This former Montecito resident—who was often seen unpretentiously shopping at local boutiques—first went before the cameras as an infant. This print-ad "baby model" made her feature film debut at age five in director Ken Russell's *Altered States*. Her next gig came at age seven in the Steven Spielberg blockbuster *E.T. the Extra-Terrestrial*, in which she memorably played little sister Gertie, who found herself locked in a closet with an alien...both of whom screamed at the sight of each other! That role made Drew one of the most recognized child performers ever, and earned her the 1982 Young Artist Award.

She won an early Golden Globe nomination for her portrayal of a child divorcing her parents in *Irreconcilable Differences*, and after revealing her early struggles with the demands of fame in her autobiography *Little Girl Lost*, Barrymore made the move to lead roles in *Poison Ivy*, *Bad Girls*, *The Wedding Singer*, and *50 First Dates*.

In 1995 Barrymore founded her own production company, Flower Films, and produced hits like *Never Been Kissed*, *Charlie's Angels*, *50 First Dates*, and *Beverly Hills Chihuahua*. The success of these movies firmly established her in the top ranks of Hollywood producers and superstars.

In her "off" time, Drew is a frequent host of *Turner Classic Movies' The Essentials with Robert Osborne*, and has been guest host of NBC-TV's *Saturday Night Live* multiple times. A Cover Girl model and spokeswoman, she made it to No. 1 on *People* magazine's 100 Most Beautiful People list, and occasionally works as a guest photographer for magazines around the world.

With appearances in more than fifty feature films winning her nearly every possible award under the sun—including a star on the Hollywood Walk of Fame—Barrymore somehow finds time to support a wide range of humanitarian causes. She currently serves the United Nations World Food Program as its Ambassador Against Hunger.

Drew Barrymore is genuine Hollywood royalty, an admired professional, and has never been afraid to openly share her feelings, admitting that "I love hugging."

WHERE HOLLYWOOD HIDES

Academy Award-winning actor, musician, cartoonist, photographer, Jeff Bridges is a longtime area resident and truly one of Santa Barbara's celebrity golden boys.

Graced with a natural, casual persona, Bridges is just as likely to be seen strolling the quiet streets of his Montecito neighborhood as dodging the crush of paparazzi on the red carpet at the Academy Awards. In either setting, Jeff Bridges is the same unpretentious guy.

Bridges and his actor brother Beau grew up in the middle of the Hollywood scene, appearing as children with their mother Dorothy Bridges in the 1951 film *The Company She Keeps*, and with their father on his hit TV series *Sea Hunt*. Jeff's first major break came in *The Last Picture Show,* for which he received an Academy Award nomination for Best Actor in a Supporting Role.

He received a second Best Actor nomination for his work in *Thunderbolt and Lightfoot*, playing opposite Clint Eastwood; he next explored a wide variety of character types in *Tron, Starman, Against All Odds, Jagged Edge, Fearless,* and *True Grit.*

The rest of his filmography embraces some unforgettable films: *Bad Company. The Last American Hero. The Iceman Cometh. Rancho Deluxe. Stay Hungry. King Kong. Winter Kills. Cutter's Way. Kiss Me Goodbye. 8 Million Ways to Die. Nadine. Tucker: The Man and His Dream. The Fabulous Baker Boys. The Fisher King. American Heart. Wild Bill. White Squall. The Big Lebowski. Arlington Road. The Contender. K-PAX. Seabiscuit. Iron Man. Crazy Heart* (for which he won the Oscar for Best Actor in a Leading Role). As Bridges himself once described his career, he "never went down that movie star path and just took the 90-degree turn from the last thing."

Jeff's musical bent nearly eclipsed his acting ambitions; before his film career really took off, he was seriously distracted by the temptation of a songwriting troubadour's life. Even today, Jeff Bridges and his band ("The Abiders") play on the road whenever he can break away from studio soundstages.

Having moved from Los Angeles to Montecito nearly thirty years ago to raise his family far from the distractions of the Hollywood lifestyle, he sums up his career with typically casual aplomb: "Well, you know...ups and downs. What does the Dude say? Strikes and gutters, man. That's about it."

JEFF BRIDGES

"Crazy Heart"

JACKSON BROWNE

Activist Songwriter

This longtime Santa Barbara ranch owner may be as well-known for his environmental and social activism as he is for his incredible music career.

Jackson Browne is simply one of the most prolific singer-songwriters of his generation or any other, with a long string of chart-topping hits to his name, including "Doctor My Eyes," "Take It Easy," "Here Come Those Tears Again," "Running on Empty," "You Love the Thunder", "That Girl Could Sing," "Somebody's Baby," "Tender is the Night," "You're a Friend of Mine...and dozens more that are heard on the radio, all day, every day.

Inducted into both the Rock and Roll Hall of Fame as well as the Songwriters Hall of Fame, Browne's career began as a Los Angeles teen warbling folk music in 1960s-era showcases like the Troubador and the Ash Grove. Just out of high school, he joined the Nitty Gritty Dirt Band, the group that recorded his "These Days" and "Shadow Dream Song." Even before he turned eighteen, he was seriously entrenched in the music business, working as a staff writer for Elektra Records. But songwriting was clearly his calling, and he soon saw his songs recorded by a wide range of talents from Gregg Allman to Joan Baez to Linda Ronstadt.

Browne is as well-known for his social activism as for his music, and his 1986 album *Lives in the Balance* artfully championed his social awareness.

When he visits his Santa Barbara ranch, Browne occasionally headlines informal on-the-beach concert fundraisers to support the community's ongoing efforts to conserve our unique natural beauty.

Environmental activist, agent for social awareness, and unmatched musical artist...Jackson Browne is a brilliant gem among Santa Barbara's many citizen-treasures.

Television, stage, and motion picture legend Carol Burnett came to Santa Barbara after a career spanning five decades as perhaps the most multifaceted on-screen female talent of the twentieth century.

Carol was born in San Antonio, Texas, and when her mother was hired as a studio publicity writer, they moved to Hollywood. After graduating from Hollywood High School, Carol left her journalism studies at UCLA and moved to New York to pursue her onstage dreams.

In pursuit of an acting career, Carol endured more than a full year of auditions and rejections, surviving on odd jobs until she won a minor role on *The Paul Winchell and Jerry Mahoney Show*, a popular afternoon children's series. Playing the comedy foil to the show's "star" Jerry Mahoney—a wooden dummy voiced by ventriloquist Paul Winchell—her convincing performance won the attention of New York and Hollywood writers and producers.

Carol eventually starred in no fewer than sixty television series, movies, and specials, from *Stanley* with Buddy Hackett in 1956 to *American Masters Tribute to Carol Burnett* in 2007. While amassing a career's worth of acting credits, Carol managed to create and produce eleven years of the most successful variety show in television history, *The Carol Burnett Show*, which won twenty-three Emmys.

Carol continues to amass television, feature film, and legitimate theater performing credits ranging from *Pete 'n' Tillie* and *The Front Page* to *Annie*, where her portrayal of Miss Hannigan carried the multi-million-dollar production to ten Academy Award nominations.

Her autobiography *One More Time* details her personal history and her industry-changing lawsuit against the *National Enquirer*, while her most recent book, *This Time Together: Laughter and Reflection*, enjoyed major success on the New York Times best-seller list.

Always gracious and open to her legions of fans, Carol has been the recipient of the 2003 Kennedy Center Honors, the Presidential Medal of Freedom, and has her star on the Hollywood Walk of Fame.

Carol now lives in Montecito, enjoying the exclusive community's perfect climate, tranquility, and a culture of celebrity privacy not found anywhere else.

CAROL BURNETT

Queen of Comedy

CHARLIE

He may have only stood five feet five inches tall, but few celebrities with genuine ties to Santa Barbara can match the show business stature of the "Little Tramp," Charlie Chaplin.

Born Charles Spencer Chaplin in 1889 England, his career as comic, mime, actor, film director, producer, screenwriter, and composer spanned more than seventy years, starting on British music hall variety stages and enduring as a Hollywood legend.

Charlie Chaplin became perhaps the most influential filmmaker in history, and is considered by the American Film Institute's rankings the tenth greatest screen legend of all time.

Young Charlie first came to America at the age of twenty-one with the Fred Karno troupe, a band of variety performers in which Charlie developed the character of The Little Tramp, his lasting trademark.

This was the era when Santa Barbara was the pre-Hollywood capital of American silent film production, and where more than a thousand movies were made. It became the playground for Hollywood royalty like Mary Pickford, Douglas Fairbanks, Jr., D.W. Griffith, and Chaplin, all of whom would become the driving force behind United Artists Studios.

By the mid-1920s, Chaplin and his celebrity friends determined that Santa Barbara needed first-class weekend accommodations, so a group of investors was brought together to build a place suitable for their needs, and the Montecito Inn was born. Since its opening, The Montecito Inn has remained a stopover for celebrities and weekend travelers, and still bears a logo featuring the likeness of the Little Tramp.

Chaplin won five Oscars throughout his career, directed seventy-five films, wrote sixty screenplays, edited fifty movies, produced thirty-five films, and personally scored the music for twenty movies...making him perhaps the most prolific of all Santa Barbara's celebrities.

WHERE HOLLYWOOD HIDES

This author of nearly twenty best-sellers was also a TV star, a recipient of the French Legion of Honor, and was awarded the U.S. Presidential Medal of Freedom. Julia Child brought all of her international celebrity with her when she came to Santa Barbara.

Julia attended Smith College, became an advertising copywriter in New York City, and during World War II found herself working in the Office of Strategic Services as a mid-level international intelligence officer. She covered various stations throughout Europe and Asia, and was even awarded the Emblem of Meritorious Civilian Service as head of her OSS office in China.

It was at that time that Julia met and married Paul Child, a U.S. Foreign Service officer who had earlier lived in Paris as an artist and poet. When Paul introduced Julia to the subtleties of French cuisine, she found her way to Paris' Le Cordon Bleu cooking school. Her fascination with all things culinary ultimately led to the publication of her encyclopedic 734-page *Mastering the Art of French Cooking*.

The book became a huge best-seller, and her appearance on an otherwise dull PBS book-review show—where she exuded her unpretentious joy in "more butter," and her infectious good humor—led to her own series, *The French Chef*. The popularity of the show—which aired long before today's cable-TV cooking channels—won her multiple Peabody and Emmy awards over its decade-long run.

Throughout her television career, Julia Child continued to write cookbooks, founded The American Institute of Wine & Food, and managed to pen the story with *My Life in France*. Her story was so unique and colorful that it became the subject of 2009's Oscar-nominated movie *Julie & Julia,* starring Amy Adams.

When Julia came to settle in Santa Barbara, she took on the role of high priestess of *haute cuisine* and prided herself on discovering the most charming nooks and crannies of the Mission City.

When asked why she chose Santa Barbara as her home, Julia summed it all up perfectly: "People just seem friendly and happy here," she wrote. "Who wouldn't be, when it's so beautiful and the climate is so nice? Why live anywhere else?"

WHERE HOLLYWOOD HIDES

JULIA CHILD

"More Butter"

JOHN CLEESE

"And now for something completely different!"

Actor, comedian, author, and educator, John Cleese stands head and shoulders above anyone of average height and comic sensibility. After all, among the pantheon of Hollywood celebrities, who but Cleese can boast of having a species of lemur *and* an astronomical asteroid named for himself?

Moving quickly beyond the constraints of a typical British education, Cleese was studying law at Cambridge University when he discovered the allure of applause as a member of the Cambridge University Footlights Revue.

What the legal profession lost, the world of comedy gained. Cleese's talents as both performer and writer of Britain's *The Frost Report* led him to create new styles of comedy that would see him through fifty-two film and television roles, an Academy Award for Best Screenplay (*A Fish Called Wanda*), and four Emmys.

After an early appearance on *The Ed Sullivan Show*, Cleese went on to create, write, and star in the classic television series *Fawlty Towers*, then to co-writing and/or performing in *Monty Python and the Holy Grail, Monty Python's Life of Brian, Monty Python's The Meaning of Life, The Great Muppet Caper, Silverado, A Fish Called Wanda, Harry Potter and the Chamber of Secrets,* and *The World Is Not Enough.*

Perhaps best known as "the tall guy from Monty Python's Flying Circus," John Cleese has long been associated with a brilliant comic sensibility arising from a deadpan humor centered on some of life's most annoying people and irritating circumstances.

Cleese has often appeared at Santa Barbara's many charitable events, and has walked (dare we say "silly walking"?) the red carpet at the Santa Barbara International Film Festival.

Throughout his years in Santa Barbara, Cleese has remained a raconteur with a razor's edge. As he famously said, "You don't have to be the Dalai Lama to tell people that life's about change."

Actor, producer, director, singer, musician, and entrepreneur, Kevin Costner has been a longtime Santa Barbara local, preferring the low-key elegance and privacy of his Carpinteria home to the hustle of Hollywood.

A Southern California native with a business degree from Cal State Fullerton, to this day Costner credits a chance meeting with the legendary Richard Burton as his acting inspiration. After that conversation, Costner devoted himself to his acting and began making the rounds to every possible Hollywood audition.

His first on-screen moments were hardly memorable (*Malibu Hot Summer, Chasing Dreams, Frances, Table for Five*), and frequently ended up on the proverbial cutting-room floor, although parts of his body were actually seen as a mortician's subject in 1983's *The Big Chill*.

Costner eventually came to public attention with a plum role in 1985's *Silverado*, playing a charming gunslinger. It was a breakout performance, and was quickly followed by roles in *Fandango, American Flyers*, Steven Spielberg's *Amazing Stories*, and Brian De Palma's *The Untouchables*.

Costner then played opposite Gene Hackman in the thriller *No Way Out*, and won the lead role in the classic baseball opus, *Bull Durham*. His portrayal of a veteran baseball catcher won the film *Sports Illustrated* magazine's nod as the #1 Greatest Sports Movie of all time.

His next baseball film, *Field of Dreams*, has been recognized by the American Film Institute as one of the top ten classics of all time. He then turned to directing with the epic *Dances with Wolves*, winning seven Academy Awards, including a pair for Costner himself for Best Picture (producer) and Best Director.

Other prominent films followed, including *Revenge, Robin Hood: Prince of Thieves, JFK, The Bodyguard, A Perfect World, Wyatt Earp, The Postman* (which he directed), *Waterworld*, and *Tin Cup*. The following decade saw him starring in *Thirteen Days, Open Range* (directing again), *The Guardian*, and *Swing Vote*. Costner's latest work has him in the sports world once again with the lead role in *Draft Day*.

Graced with humility and creative brilliance, Kevin Costner is a multifaceted entrepreneur, artist, and humanitarian who has appeared on the red carpet at the Santa Barbara International Film Festival before…and will certainly be there again.

KEVIN COSTNER

"Field of Dreams"

DAVID CROSBY

Crosby, Stills, & Nash

In the world of classic rock era music, the talent and career of Santa Barbara denizen David Crosby stands at the top of any list of "greats."

As a founding member of The Byrds and later of Crosby, Stills, & Nash, few Santa Barbarans can match Crosby's impact on American pop culture. The list of hit songs this guitarist and singer can claim is impressive: "Fifth Dimension," "Younger Than Yesterday," "Farther Along," "Just a Song Before I Go," "Wind on the Water," "Heart of Gold," "Turn! Turn! Turn!"…and the list goes on and on.

Crosby's parents (his father was Floyd Crosby, an Academy Award-winning cinematographer) brought him and his brother Ethan to Santa Barbara to raise them away from the hustle and bustle of showbiz. After attending local area schools and a short stint at Santa Barbara City College, by 1960 Crosby's interest in music and guitar had him playing in local clubs more than attending to academics.

When Crosby partnered with another folk singer, Roger McGuinn, the two began playing folk music using electric guitars and amplification. Crosby and McGuinn brought Chris Hillman, Gene Clark, and Michael Clarke together to form the The Byrds. Their first release, a cover of Bob Dylan's "Mr. Tambourine Man," went to the top of the charts. That was quickly followed by a succession of wildly popular albums…all led by the dynamic, creative instincts of David Crosby.

When The Byrds broke up, Crosby went on to collaborate with then-unknowns Joni Mitchell and Neil Young, as well as with established performers Stephen Stills of Buffalo Springfield and Graham Nash of The Hollies. Eventually, it was the combined talents of Crosby, Stills, and Nash that led to Crosby's greatest impact on the music scene. The legendary Woodstock festival of 1969, in which Crosby, Stills, and Nash played before a half-million fans, marked the epicenter of the Sixties Revolution, forever marking Crosby's place in American pop culture.

WHERE HOLLYWOOD HIDES

Ranked among the world's most powerful celebrities, Tom Cruise made an impressive journey from his childhood in Syracuse, New York, to the rarefied world of show business stardom as one of Hollywood's most bankable actors.

Having attended fifteen schools by the time he entered high school, Tom's natural athletic abilities and early interest in studying for the priesthood eventually took a back seat to his overwhelming commitment to the performing arts. When he was put on his high school wrestling team's injured list, he auditioned for and won the lead in the school's production of Guys and Dolls. With the roar of his classmates' applause ringing in his ears, his future course was set.

Like many actor-superstars before him, Cruise left academics behind for the school of hard knocks and endless auditions. He headed for New York and quickly began finding film work, debuting in Endless Love (starring Brooke Shields), then winning a mid-level part in Taps, working alongside George C. Scott and Sean Penn. More roles quickly followed with Francis Coppola's The Outsiders, followed by his breakout role as Joel Goodsen in Risky Business.

His performances since are the stuff of Hollywood box office history: Top Gun. The Color of Money. Rain Main. Born on the Fourth of July. Interview with the Vampire. Mission Impossible. Vanilla Sky. Minority Report. War of the Worlds. The Last Samurai. Jerry Maguire...and the list continues to grow.

Voted repeatedly as one of the "100 Sexiest Stars" and ranked high on the list of "The Top 100 Movies Stars of All Time," Cruise is frequently chosen by People magazine as "one of the 50 most beautiful people in the world."

Once his footing was established as Hollywood's #1 box office attraction, Cruise parlayed his power into the role of prominent and prolific film producer. Through his Cruise/Wagner Productions, he's won the Nova Award as Most Promising Producer, the Producer's Guild of America Golden Laurel Award, and has been nominated for Motion Picture Producer of the Year. He doesn't confine himself to the "small" stories, either, as his producing debut Mission: Impossible has been followed by Vanilla Sky, The Last Samurai, and Valkyrie.

Having recently become the owner of a magnificent Montecito estate, Cruise is one of the most active Hollywood stars of his generation, with a profound interest in all world issues. Among those are a number of international charitable causes he personally supports, making Tom Cruise a true Santa Barbara superstar.

WHERE HOLLYWOOD HIDES

TOM CRUISE

Hollywood's "Top Gun"

DOUG DAVIDSON

"The Young & the Restless"

It's a rare Hollywood actor who can lay claim to having played the same role without interruption for more than three decades, but longtime Santa Barbara resident Doug Davidson has managed to do exactly that as the male lead in CBS-TV's *The Young and the Restless*.

While just a high school freshman, Doug became interested in acting and did some early catalogue modeling, even appearing in a Fruit of the Loom ad campaign with future *Baywatch* star David Hasselhoff.

He enrolled in Occidental College as a marine biology major, but soon turned all of his energies toward theater arts. With a winning personality and great comic timing, it wasn't long until he began landing small parts in television commercials.

Davidson's commercial work led to small roles in a handful of films, including *Fraternity Row*, *Mr. Write*, *Dreaming of Joseph Lees*, and *Don't Stop Now*. His early television work at that time included supporting roles in ABC's *The Initiation of Sarah* and in CBS' *I'll Take Manhattan*.

When Doug accompanied a friend to the set of *The Young and the Restless*, he was invited to audition for a small guest role, which led to a short string of brief appearances on the show. Realizing that Davidson had an unusual energy and leading man appeal, the producers created the character of private investigator Paul Williams just for him...and he did not disappoint, quickly pulling in his own fan base to the show.

More than thirty years later, the rest—as they say—is showbiz history. Davidson went on to be named Outstanding Hero by *Soap Opera Digest*, has been nominated for the Emmy as Outstanding Daytime Lead Actor, and has become a perennial choice as host for a wide variety of media events. Doug has been the host of the nighttime version of *The Price Is Right*, served as master of ceremonies for the *Kenny Rogers Cerebral Palsy Telethon* and the *Miss California Pageant*, has hosted the *Tournament of Roses Parade*, and with the exception of the show's host, holds the record for appearances on *Family Feud*.

With *The Young and the Restless* still television's No. 1 daytime show, Doug Davidson's popularity with his fans remains a sure thing.

Geena Davis is unique among Hollywood superstars in that she didn't really get started as a working actor until she was well into her twenties.

Her statuesque height served her well as a New York fashion model and led to her being cast by director Sydney Pollack alongside Dustin Hoffman in 1982's *Tootsie*. That role brought her to the attention of major Hollywood casting agents, and as the glowing reviews were just coming in, she was immediately offered the role of Wendy Killian in NBC's *Buffalo Bill*, playing opposite Dabney Coleman and Joanna Cassidy.

Even as she was gaining a huge following on that show, Davis was in demand by several other hit shows, appearing in guest starring roles on *Knight Rider*, *Riptide*, *Remington Steele*, and her own starring series, *Sara*.

Her popularity on television gave her the added momentum to dive into the worlds of comedy and sci-fi, playing opposite Chevy Chase in *Fletch*, then appearing in *Beetlejuice* and *The Fly*. She followed that by winning the Academy Award as Best Supporting Actress for her work in *The Accidental Tourist*.

Shortly thereafter, Geena's iconic role in 1991's classic *Thelma & Louise* won her the Best Actress Golden Globe Award. Her portrayal of Thelma Dickinson was widely acclaimed, winning her an Academy Award nomination as Best Actress. She filled out the decade with major performances in *A League of Their Own*, *Hero*, *Speechless*, *Cutthroat Island*, *The Long Kiss Goodnight*, *Stuart Little*, and *Commander in Chief* (playing the first female U.S. president, and winning another Best Actress Golden Globe).

Beyond her impressive body of film work, Geena became intrigued by the sport of archery, and actually came close to winning a berth on the 2000 U.S. Olympic team.

As a social activist, Geena Davis is a force to be reckoned with, having founded the Geena Davis Institute on Gender in Media and winning an honorary Ph.D. for her media research and leadership role in the Women's Sports Foundation.

Geena Davis, at one time a resident of Montecito, is a true Santa Barbara adventurer whose career proves what she has famously said: "If you risk nothing, then you risk everything."

WHERE HOLLYWOOD HIDES

GEENA DAVIS

In a league of her own...

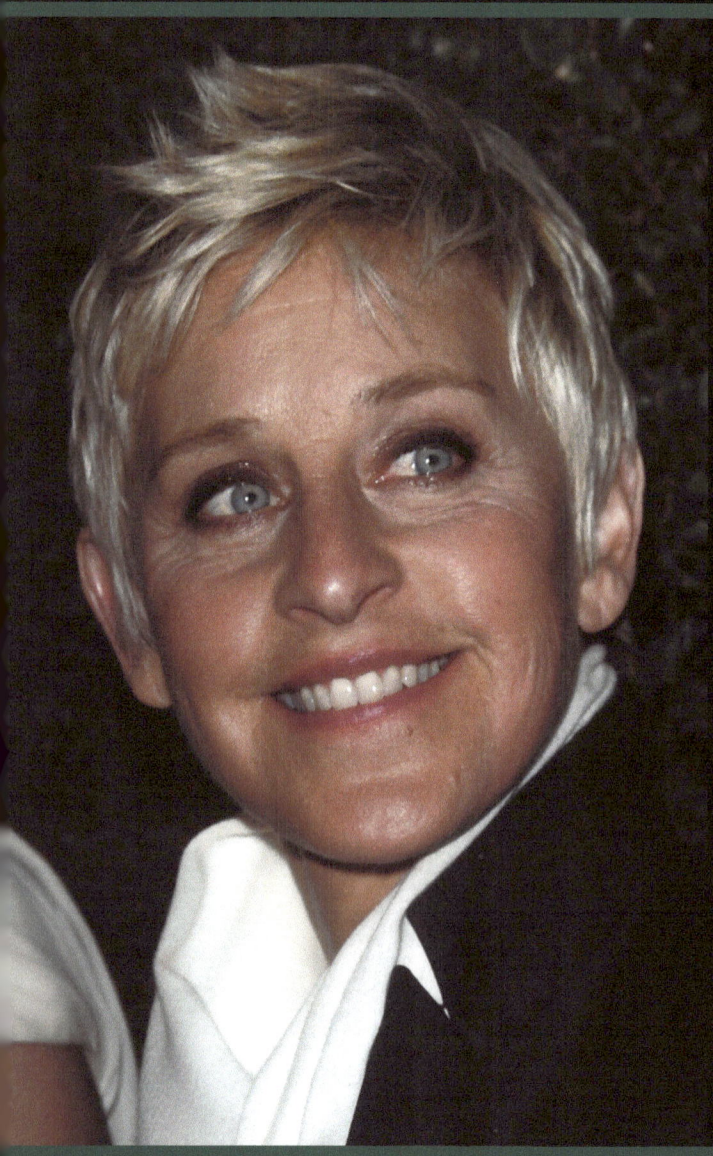

ELLEN DEGENERES

"Procrastination is not the problem. It's the solution."

Stand-up comic, film actress, sitcom star, talk show host, *Time* magazine cover subject, animated voiceover artist, commercial spokeswoman, *American Idol* judge, and outspoken social activist, Ellen DeGeneres has managed to fit into Santa Barbara's casual lifestyle like no other.

Ellen discovered her comedic bent early in life. At the age of thirteen, she took it upon herself to cheer up her recently divorced mother and quickly realized the power of her comedy instincts. She was the emcee at Clyde's Comedy Club in New Orleans when she began to tour nationally, and quickly attracted media attention. Her first personal monologue, "A Phone Call to God," eventually won her Showtime's Funniest Person in America award.

It was her appearance with Johnny Carson on NBC's *Tonight Show* that brought her to national public attention. Following her brief stand-up bit, Carson invited her to join him at his desk, making Ellen the first female comic in *Tonight Show* history to ever make it to "the couch."

DeGeneres suddenly found herself awash in new opportunities, and joined the cast of Fox Television's *Open House*. Film roles quickly came her way, with appearances in *Coneheads*, *Mr. Wrong*, *Goodbye Lover*, and *EDtv*.

Ellen found her true character niche with the ABC sitcom *Ellen*, which became a smash hit, winning her an Emmy and Golden Globe Awards.

She then defied all odds with *The Ellen DeGeneres Show*, a daytime talk show where she revealed her deadpan timing and relatable persona...qualities which have helped the show win twenty-five Emmys.

Ellen has been embraced by her audience even further, as she makes frequent appearances in national ad campaigns and has been seen as spokesperson for American Express and Cover Girl Cosmetics, and recently held center stage as host of the *Academy Awards*.

Smart, funny, and as real as it gets, this dog lover is a frequent Santa Barbaran. If you've got a dog, take a walk on any of the local beaches. You might bump into another dog lover who just happens to be a media mogul...by the name of Ellen.

WHERE HOLLYWOOD HIDES

From teenage model to motion picture superstar, *Playboy* magazine cover girl, television series lead, and international animal rights activist, Bo Derek's celebrity footprint stands solidly and squarely on Santa Barbara soil.

Her first film role in 1977's *Orca* brought Bo to the attention of director Blake Edwards, who cast her opposite Dudley Moore in a role that propelled her to instant sex-symbol stardom. Her performance as a "10," won her a Golden Globe nomination for New Star of The Year.

She followed that with *Tarzan, the Ape Man,* and with the first of several featured appearances in the pages of *Playboy*.

Her performance as Ryan O'Neal's wife in *Malibu's Most Wanted*, as well as roles in *Fashion House*, *Two Guys and a Girl*, *Boom*, *Life in the Balance*, *Queen of Swords*, *Murder at the Cannes Film Festival*, *Wind on Water*, *The Drew Carey Show*, and *Tommy Boy* have firmly established her as an actress who has managed to surpass her physical beauty to reveal true acting prowess.

Bo is a serious rider and breeder of Iberian horses and has appeared at numerous Santa Barbara equestrian charity events where she lends her name and voice to the causes in which she believes strongly.

Bo serves on the California Horse Racing Board and as national honorary chairperson for Veterans Affairs' National Rehabilitation Special Events. Her advocacy for wounded veterans earned her the Veterans Administration's highest honors and an Honorary Green Beret from U.S. Special Forces. Bo Derek's consistent public service nearly overshadows her on-screen accomplishments.

But at the end of the day, when the business of Hollywood and activism and politics are set aside, there is no place Bo would rather be than out for a ride on one of her gorgeous horses. How committed is she to the equestrian life? She herself said it best in the title of her own autobiography: *Everything That Matters in Life I Learned from Horses*.

BO DEREK

A Perfect "10"

KIRK DOUGLAS

True Hollywood Royalty

Kirk Douglas, a longtime resident of Montecito, is veteran of more than eighty feature films, having portrayed some of contemporary cinema's most memorable characters. He's received Academy Award nominations as Best Actor in three classic films (*Champion*, *The Bad and the Beautiful*, *Lust for Life*), and was awarded an Honorary Academy Award in 1995 for the totality of his lifelong work.

Douglas' early acting ambitions were postponed by the outbreak of World War II, which saw him commissioned as a Navy ensign chasing enemy submarines. Injured in combat, he was medically discharged in 1944 and returned to the acting life.

What followed is legendary: in rapid succession, he won roles in *Kiss and Tell*, *The Strange Love of Martha Ivers*, *Out of the Past*, *Mourning Becomes Electra*, *The Walls of Jericho*, *My Dear Secretary*, and the film that established his powerful, gritty screen persona, *Champion*.

Douglas became an international star with films like *Lust for Life*, *Paths of Glory*, *The Vikings*, and *Spartacus*. With the vision to form his own production company, he produced and starred in *Seven Days in May*, *The List of Adrian Messenger*, and *The Indian Fighter*. Douglas personally challenged the McCarthy-era Hollywood blacklist and brought it to an end by hiring writers and directors no studio would touch.

More memorable roles followed in classics like *Lonely re the Brave*, *In Harm's Way*, *Cast a Giant Shadow*, *Is Paris Burning?*, *The War Wagon*, *The Brotherhood*, *Dr. Jekyll and Mr. Hyde*, *Posse* (which he directed), *The Man from Snowy River*, *Eddie Macon's Run*, *Tough Guys*, and *Inherit the Wind*…to highlight only a few.

Kirk Douglas is the author of no fewer than eleven books, an internationally recognized art collector, and has been widely hailed for his devotion to humanitarian causes and personal philanthropy. He's been an official Goodwill Ambassador for the U.S. State Department, was awarded the Presidential Medal of Freedom, received the Jefferson Award, France's Chevalier of the Legion of Honor, the American Cinema Award, the National Board of Reviews Career Achievement Award, the Screen Actors Guild Lifetime Achievement Award, the Kennedy Center Honors Lifetime Achievement Award, and the American Film Institute's Lifetime Achievement Award.

In speaking of his remarkable work habits, passion, and commitment to his craft, Douglas says, "All you can do in life is try."

By any standard, Kirk Douglas has done more than try. He succeeded like no other.

Celebrities don't come any more Santa Barbara-centric than UCSB alumnus Michael Douglas.

With the family name as a calling card, Michael's first film role—while still an undergrad—was in a bit part in 1966's *Cast a Giant Shadow*, which starred his father Kirk alongside Yul Brynner, John Wayne, and Frank Sinatra.

After graduating with a B.A. in theater arts, Michael was cast as the lead in *Hail, Hero!*, a role that won him a Golden Globe Award for Most Promising Male Newcomer. More work followed with the title role in *Adam at Six A.M.*, followed by *Summertree*, and then a co-starring role in *Napoleon and Samantha*.

He jumped at the opportunity to play Karl Malden's young sidekick in the ABC-TV hit cop show *The Streets of San Francisco*, which firmly established Michael as an action-capable star. His relationship with Malden went beyond the merely professional, with each man holding the other in highest personal regard. When they appeared together at the 1996 *People's Choice Awards*, Malden publicly called Douglas "the son I never had."

During the final year of *Streets*, Michael produced *One Flew Over the Cuckoo's Nest*, only the second movie in history (*It Happened One Night* with Clark Gable was the first). Not bad for a first-time producer!

Douglas then starred in more than thirty hit films, including *Coma, Running, The China Syndrome* (which he also produced), *The Star Chamber, Romancing the Stone, A Chorus Line, The Jewel of the Nile, Fatal Attraction, Wall Street, Basic Instinct, Wonder Boys, Solitary Man, Traffic, Haywire,* and the critically-acclaimed HBO film *Behind the Candelabra*, featuring his uncanny portrayal of flamboyant pianist Liberace.

Having lived in Santa Barbara and Montecito for more than thirty years, he established the Douglas Family Preserve, a 70-acre park named to honor his father Kirk. He also established the UCSB Center for Film, Television, and New Media, making his mark on the community indelible. "I love UCSB, and am proud to be associated with it," he said when his funding was announced.

Michael Douglas is a genuine Hollywood star, a magnanimous Santa Barbara community supporter, and a true class act.

MICHAEL DOUGLAS

"One Flew Over the Cuckoo's Nest"

ANTHONY EDWARDS

A Santa Barbara Native Son

Santa Barbara may not be the Big Apple or even the Big Orange, but with a local population of only plus-or-minus 100,000 souls, the area has given the world more than its fair share of successful Hollywood stars.

Anthony Edwards is among the city's boys who "made good." Born in Santa Barbara, Edwards was raised in the hillside Riviera neighborhood, the youngest of four kids. With artistically-inclined parents—his father was an architect, his mother a landscape painter—his early acting ambitions were given free reign and he began performing in local shows at the age of twelve, making his first stage appearance in the Santa Barbara Youth Theatre production of *Peter Pan*.

While at San Marcos High School, Edwards was known for his commitment to the arts by his study of ballet...although he later confessed it had merely been a ruse to meet girls. By the time he graduated from high school, he'd established his thespian *bona fides* by appearing in more than thirty plays.

After studying at London's Royal Academy of Dramatic Art and USC, he began receiving offers for professional roles, the first of which was in CBS-TV's *The Killing of Randy Webster*. With this first credit under his belt, Edwards went on to the ABC sitcom *It Takes Two*, which was quickly followed by his being cast in *Fast Times at Ridgemont High*.

His first shot at playing a leading role came in 1985's *Gotcha*, which was quickly followed by *The Sure Thing*, and then his career-making portrayal of Goose as Tom Cruise's sidekick in *Top Gun*. That performance was followed in rapid succession by work in *Revenge of the Nerds II*, *Miracle Mile*, *Mr. North*, *Pet Sematary Two*, *Delta Heat*, *Sexual Healing*, and *The Client*.

While working in movies, Edwards was also a sought-after television performer and appeared in *Walking Tall*, *Police Squad*, *High School U.S.A.*, and *Northern Exposure*. Then Edwards was cast in NBC-TV's *ER* in the memorable role of Dr. Mark Greene, winning five Screen Actors Guild Awards, a Golden Globe, and multiple Emmy nominations.

Edwards also has an impressive track record as a director and producer, winning the Carnegie Medal for Excellence in Children's Video as well as the Daytime Emmy for Outstanding Children's Special for *My Louisiana Sky*.

Edwards spends most of his time in New York now, but Santa Barbara is proud to call this homegrown Hollywood star a true native son.

WHERE HOLLYWOOD HIDES

The role of the music composer, while one of those "invisible" skills, is every bit as fundamental to the success of any movie or TV show as that of its actors or directors, and Santa Barbara local Danny Elfman surely belongs in the pantheon of musical superstars.

Born and raised in Los Angeles, Danny left his high school band behind before even graduating, to travel with his violin throughout Europe and Africa. After returning home, he joined his brother Richard's musical theater troupe, The Mystic Knights of the Oingo Boingo, which eventually morphed into the rock group Oingo Boingo. It was with his brother that Danny created his first film score for Richard Elfman's feature film, *Forbidden Zone*.

Then, in 1985, Tim Burton and Paul Reubens recruited Elfman to create the music for an off-the-wall comedy they were working on called *Pee-wee's Big Adventure*. The Burton–Elfman friendship evolved, with Danny going on to create the soundtrack for such Burton classics as *Beetlejuice*, *Batman*, *Batman Returns*, *Edward Scissorhands*, *Mars Attacks!*, *Sleepy Hollow*, *Planet of the Apes*, *Spider-Man 2*, *Charlie and the Chocolate Factory*, *Corpse Bride*, and *Alice in Wonderland*. When he's not working with Burton, Elfman has managed to find time to score the music for no fewer than two dozen other major films for directors Richard Donner (*Scrooged*), Warren Beatty (*Dick Tracy*), Brian De Palma (*Mission: Impossible*), and Gus Van Sant (*Restless*).

Elfman is also well-known as "the master of the theme song," having created well over a dozen film and television themes, for shows ranging from *Sledge Hammer!* and *The Simpsons* to *Desperate Housewives*.

Danny Elfman has won four Academy Award nominations, more than two dozen BMI Film & Television Awards, a Grammy, multiple Golden Globes, and numerous Film Critics Association Awards.

One of his generation's most successful musical innovators, Elfman is that rare talent who has made the transition from genuine rock 'n' roller to genuine Hollywood creative force…all while calling Santa Barbara home.

DANNY ELFMAN
Music Superstar

MEL FERRER

Classic Swordsman and "Falcon Crest" Star

If ever there was a class act in Hollywood, Mel Ferrer was it.

Proud to have been born and bred of aristocratic Spanish and Irish lineage, Mel came from a distinguished East Coast family. With a Nobel Prize-winning sister and a physician brother, Mel was himself the product of a Connecticut prep school and a Princeton University education.

At age twenty, he won Princeton's Theatre Intime award, and by the age of twenty-nine was directing *Cyrano de Bergerac* on Broadway. It wasn't long before Hollywood beckoned.

Early film work featured the tall, gracefully athletic young actor in *Lost Boundaries*, *Born to Be Bad*, *The Secret Fury*, *Rancho Notorious*, and *Scaramouche*, in which Ferrer and Stewart Granger engaged in a spectacular swordfight that remains the longest fencing duel in the history of cinema. Even today, the sheer athleticism displayed by Ferrer in this 1952 historical adventure—in which he performs in seven fully-staged sword fights—takes your breath away.

Gifted with a deep and incisive intellect, Mel's acting resume reflects his extraordinary and thoughtful nature, and includes roles in *Lili*, *Knights of the Round Table*, *War and Peace*, *Paris Does Strange Things*, *The Sun Also Rises*, *The World, the Flesh, and the Devil*, *The Fall of the Roman Empire*, and *El Greco*.

As he matured, Ferrer continued to be in strong demand in significant supporting roles, and in the 1970s alone he appeared in more than two dozen major films while producing the acclaimed suspense thriller *Wait Until Dark,* which starred Audrey Hepburn, to whom he was then married. The film won rave reviews, and to this day ranks at #55 on the American Film Institute's "100 Thrills" list.

But it was a television role that cemented the image of the cultured Mel Ferrer in the mind of audiences worldwide. Phillip Erickson of CBS-TV's *Falcon Crest*, the man who won the hand and heart of Jane Wyman's Angela Channing, will be forever remembered as the most charismatic "older man" in a network television series.

Ferrer retired to his beloved Carpinteria ranch, but he never stopped working. A master horticulturist, he was far more than just another gentleman farmer. As he had been on the stages of Princeton and Broadway…as he had been on the soundstages of Hollywood…as he was when working his twenty acres overlooking the Pacific, Mel Ferrer was never satisfied with anything less than complete mastery of his domain.

Jane Fonda was bitten by the acting bug at the age of seventeen, when she first appeared with her father Henry at the Omaha Community Playhouse in a charity production of *The Country Girl*.

Leaving her studies at Vassar, Jane went to New York to focus on her acting ambitions at Lee Strasberg's Actors Studio. Her passion and discipline led her quickly from the stage to a dynamic film career, which began with her appearance in *Tall Story*.

Hollywood was receptive to her intelligence and lithe beauty, and she quickly won roles in *Period of Adjustment* and *Walk on the Wild Side*, which earned her the Golden Globe as Most Promising Newcomer. Just a few years later, a major career breakthrough came with the classic comedy *Cat Ballou*, quickly followed by *Any Wednesday* and then *Barefoot in the Park* opposite Robert Redford.

She became a true sex symbol in the sci-fi spoof *Barbarella*, and then reversed course when she promptly won an Oscar nomination for her performance in *They Shoot Horses, Don't They?*, followed by an Oscar win in *Klute*.

A tireless work ethic propelled Jane through a series of feature films, including *A Doll's House*, *Steelyard Blues*, *The Blue Bird*, *Fun with Dick and Jane*, *Julia* (for which she received another Best Actress Nomination), and *Coming Home*, the quintessential Vietnam era anti-war film.

Major successes continued with her work in *The China Syndrome*, *The Electric Horseman*, *Nine to Five*, *On Golden Pond*, *The Dollmaker*, *Agnes of God*, *Stanley & Iris*, and *Monster-in-Law*.

While building this impressive list of major film credits, Fonda used her boundless energies to become an international fitness guru. Her *Workout Starring Jane Fonda* went on to create an entire industry in exercise videos, and has sold nearly 20 million copies.

As well as her multiple Oscars, Golden Globes, and Emmys, this former resident of Laurel Springs Ranch in the Santa Barbara foothills has been named a United Nations Goodwill Ambassador, received the Cannes Film Festival Palme d'Or, and is a member of the California Hall of Fame.

JANE FONDA

Oscar Winning "Workout Queen"

JOHN FORSYTHE

From "Bachelor Father" to "Dynasty"

Bentley Gregg. Charlie Townsend. Blake Carrington. Three unforgettable roles, all played by John Forsythe, one of Hollywood's true gentlemen.

During the Golden Age of Television, Forsythe's square-jawed good looks and unique vocal tones won him a variety of guest starring roles on shows like *Alfred Hitchcock Presents*, *Kraft Television Theatre*, *Robert Montgomery Presents*, *Schlitz Playhouse*, and *The Philco Television Playhouse*.

Forsythe was cast in a role tailor-made for his patrician origins and cosmopolitan manners as the lead in CBS' *Bachelor Father*, a fan favorite that played on all three of the major networks.

He returned to feature films with appearances in *Kitten with a Whip* and *In Cold Blood*, and then was cast by TV's mega-producer Aaron Spelling as the unseen Charlie of *Charlie's Angels*. He was heard on each episode over the show's five-year ABC-TV run, giving the Angels their weekly crime-busting instructions. While working on *Charlie's Angels*, Forsythe appeared in *And Justice for All* as a sociopathic judge, and his first role as a true "heavy."

At that point, Forsythe was once again summoned by Aaron Spelling to step into shoes only he could fill: *Dynasty*'s Blake Carrington.

Always the embodiment of grace, style, and cultured class, Forsythe's portrayal of a sly and dominating Denver oil baron ultimately unseated the nighttime-soap ratings domination by *Dallas*' J.R. Ewing. Debuting as a mid-season replacement show, for four years *Dynasty* scratched and clawed its way—just as Alexis and Krystle did in their frequent catfights—to the top of the ratings heap for ABC-TV.

After a career that included twenty-five feature films and double that number of television movies, series, and specials, after having been nominated for myriad Emmys and Golden Globes, after seeing his star placed on the Hollywood Walk of Fame, Forsythe and his wife of fifty-one years retired to their gorgeous 30-acre ranch just a stone's throw from Michael Jackson's "Neverland" in the Santa Ynez Valley.

Instantly recognizable even when she walked the streets of Santa Barbara in "casual incognito" simply because of her trademark beauty spot and blue-eyed, wavy-blonde-haired good looks, this longtime local resident stood tall in the acting world of film and television for nearly six decades.

With more than forty feature films, a dozen television series, two dozen miniseries, and nearly 200 TV episodes to her credit, few performers can match the breadth and depth of Anne Francis' acting career.

Francis began working as a John Robert Powers model at the age of five, and was soon performing in radio shows and on the Broadway stage. By the age of eleven, she was acting opposite Gertrude Lawrence in 1941's *Lady in the Dark*.

It wasn't long before Hollywood came calling and, after being cast in a number of MGM "cheesecake" roles, Anne found herself working for Darryl F. Zanuck at 20th Century Fox where she appeared in *This Time for Keeps*, *Summer Holiday*, *Portrait of Jennie*, and *So Young, So Bad*. Her appearance opposite Spencer Tracy in *Bad Day at Black Rock* began to establish her as a serious actress, and her performance in 1955's *Blackboard Jungle* reinforced that industry perception.

Anne worked steadily in feature films for the next thirty years, appearing in *The Scarlet Coat*, *Forbidden Planet*, *The Great American Pastime*, *The Hired Gun*, *Don't Go Near the Water*, *The Man from U.N.C.L.E.*, *More Dead Than Alive*, *Pancho Villa*, *Agatha*, and *Funny Girl* with Barbra Streisand.

Blessed with stunning good looks and the lithe physique of a supermodel/superhero, her fan base exploded when she became ABC-TV's glamorous Honey West. One of the only female action-lead characters on television, Honey West first appeared in *Burke's Law* and earned Anne a Golden Globe for her portrayal.

Anne's life in Santa Barbara was filled with creative, charitable, and social activities, and her appearance at fundraisers always guaranteed a capacity turnout.

More than just a lifelong stunning beauty and profoundly talented performer, Anne Francis was a Santa Barbara superstar of grace and distinction.

ANNE FRANCIS

Television's First Action Heroine

DENNIS FRANZ

"NYPD Blue's"
Tough Cop

When you spot Dennis Franz walking down Santa Barbara's State Street or hanging out at the local bookstore, you might first think, "That guy looks like a cop." For this native of Chicago who has built a formidable Hollywood career portraying men with a badge, there could be no higher praise.

Franz's Emmy-winning role as Detective Andy Sipowicz in *NYPD Blue*, following his work as Lt. Norm Buntz on *Hill Street Blues*, truly cemented his law enforcement thespian persona. But those characters came to life only as the result of a lifetime of professional dedication and intensive work that has seen Dennis Franz appear in more than fifty films and television shows.

When Dennis won the lead in his high school production of *Hiawatha*, the acting bug bit him hard, and he followed his passion to study theater arts. But his career was put on hold by military service, which ultimately gave him the powerful, mature focus that has been the source of some of his most memorable characters.

Dennis broke into feature films with Robert Altman's *A Wedding*, followed by Brian De Palma's *The Fury*. With Hollywood directors and casting agents drawn to his gritty, edgy portrayals, he moved to L.A. and found himself appearing in *A Perfect Couple*, *Bleacher Bums* (which he co-wrote and earlier produced as a play), *Dressed to Kill*, *Popeye*, *Blow Out*, *Psycho II*, *Body Double*, and *Die Hard 2*.

Franz's television star rose steadily, playing the lead in *The Bay City Blues* and then joining the ensemble cast of *Hill Street Blues*. With television credits that include *The Simpsons*, *Texas Justice*, *Nasty Boys*, *Kiss Shot*, *Beverly Hills Buntz*, and *Hunter*, Franz has won four Emmys, a Golden Globe, Screen Actors Guild Awards, and he has a star on the Hollywood Walk of Fame.

Franz takes an active part in the life of the community, serving as grand marshal of the Santa Barbara Holiday Parade, and has made many personal appearances at the yearly Santa Barbara International Film Festival, where he's still recognized by fans as the toughest cop in town.

WHERE HOLLYWOOD HIDES

Santa Barbara was the seat of a thriving film industry when Hollywood and

Movies in Santa Barbara

By WALKER TOMPKINS

Two actors of the early days run through a tense scene in an old-time horse opera filmed in Santa Barbara in 1912. Then, as now, such thrillers were popular.

ONE DROWSY midsummer day in 1910, the good people of Santa Barbara were rudely shocked out of their siesta lethargy by a spurred and booted cowpuncher who galloped into town with six-guns blazing. The ensuing pandemonium was recorded for posterity by a hand-cranked movie camera mounted on a Model T flivver that bore the sign ESSANAY PICTURES, INC.

The cowboy was not arrested for disturbing the peace. Rather, the populace acclaimed him as the harbinger of a new era in the placid life of the seaside resort. For he was the "A" of Essanay: "Broncho Billy" Anderson, the Roy Rogers of his generation.

Today, forty-five years later, not one tourist in a thousand who drives up Santa Barbara's State Street to visit the historic Old Mission pays a second glance at the tile-roofed, bell-towered building at the corner of State and Mission streets. In a city where a unique building code requires harmonious Spanish architecture in everything from service stations to churches, that is understandable. The building houses a mortuary now. But when it was built, in 1913, it was California's first big movie studio, and made Santa Barbara the movie capital of the U.S.A. before Hollywood came into being.

The morning Broncho Billy made his ear-splitting debut on the somnolent Santa Barbara scene, some eighty miles away a farmer was trimming a holly hedge around his grape vineyard on the flat prairie northeast of Los Angeles. That accounted for the spot being called "Hollywood and Vine" when in later years it became a world-famous crossroads under a smoggy sun. But the birthplace of the movie industry on the West Coast was not Hollywood, but Santa Barbara.

Essanay was soon joined by other production companies—thirteen at one time—who began turning out scores of two-reel custard-pie comedies, cliffhanger serials, and Wild West horse operas.

The American Film Company, granddaddy of Metro-Goldwyn-Mayer, Twentieth Century-Fox and other modern flicker factories, erected an ornate studio at the block bounded by Mission, Padre, Chapala and State. The "Flying A," as it was called, was the largest film foundry in the world in 1913.

Film celebrities flocked into Santa Barbara. Lottie and Mary Pickford, Art Acord, Wally Reid, Kolb & Dill, Thomas H. Ince, Richard Bennett and his daughters Constance and Joan, Frank Borzage, Marian Davies, William Desmond Taylor, and many more. Chief cameraman was Roy Overbaugh. One of his assistants was a schoolboy named Victor Fleming, native of the town. Years later, Fleming was to direct the immortal classic **Gone With the Wind**, with Overbaugh as one of his photographic advisors.

Far from resenting the filmdom intruders, Santa Barbara citizens in those halcyon days hastened to "get in on the act" themselves. Half the citizens in town who are over fifty today appeared as extras in those early mob scenes, often without pay.

The Santa Barbara area, then as now, offered every type of scenery a movie mogul could ask for. The exotic palm-girt beach doubled for desert islands, the African coast, South Sea atolls. The rugged Santa Ynez mountains, sprawling high above the city, furnished three-D technicolor canyons, beetling rimrocks and hair-raising roads where almost any day of the week you could watch sheriffs chasing outlaws, or Indians stalking the United States Cavalry.

In suburban Montecito, the palatial mansions of the millionaire set offered ready-made exteriors free for the filming. They turned up on the world's theater screens posing as English manor houses, villas on the French Riviera, or exotic castles in Spain.

Who can forget the coast of Egypt and the parting of the Red Sea in America's first million-dollar epic, **The Ten Commandments**? Cecil B. DeMille filmed those shots at the Oceano Dunes, on Highway 101 in the northwestern part of Santa Barbara County.

Even then, the movies paid extravagant salaries. Big-name players cashed two thousand dollar tax-free pay checks every Friday. But the stunt men, who risked their necks and occasionally broke them, drew a paltry twenty-five dollar stipend.

On one occasion, Cameraman Overbaugh was working on a Flying A comedy that called for a tin lizzie to beat a railroad train across the Hope Ranch grade crossing on the north edge of town. The Southern Pacific declined to permit a fake race in slow motion. So the intrepid movie-makers pulled it off anyway, just as the crack Los Angeles passenger express was approaching Santa Barbara at a mile-a-minute clip.

"The flivver load of comedians got across the tracks, all right," Overbaugh recalls, "but the locomotive cowcatcher clipped off a rear fender. The narrow escape didn't faze our stunt men, but the poor engineer was so jittery he got off the train then and there and refused to finish the run to Los Angeles."

Mr. Overbaugh, now living in retirement in Santa Barbara, recalls another script that asked the stunt men to race

The history of Flying A Studios has always been a source of journalistic interest

Courtesy Santa Barbara Historical Museum

Flying A Studios' silent screen action on the back lot
Courtesy Santa Barbara Historical Museum

Instantly recognizable by her signature dreadlocks, wire-rimmed glasses, and radiant smile, Whoopi Goldberg's remarkable Hollywood career puts her at the very top of Santa Barbara's celebrity A-list.

When Whoopi discovered Santa Barbara and the Santa Ynez Valley, she moved into the neighborhood of Bo Derek, David Crosby, Jimmy Connors, and Johnny Mathis, among many others...a far cry from her childhood in Manhattan's Chelsea neighborhood where she grew up as Caryn Elaine Johnson.

The young Caryn—an indefatigable personality who led family members to describe her as a "whoopee cushion"—made it clear that she had her sights set on a showbiz career. When her mother suggested that the family name wasn't "Jewish enough" to help her break in, she assumed her unique name, and it has served her well.

Whoopi first appeared on film in *Citizen: I'm Not Losing My Mind, I'm Giving It Away*. The notoriety generated by that role inspired her monologues that became *The Spook Show*, which director Mike Nichols took to Broadway for a critically-acclaimed six-month run, catching the attention of Steven Spielberg.

Spielberg promptly cast her in *The Color Purple*, where she won her first Golden Globe. Whoopi's career has been nonstop ever since, earning a long list of stellar movie and TV credits, including *Jumpin' Jack Flash*, *Burglar*, *Fatal Beauty*, *The Telephone*, *Clara's Heart*, *Beverly Hills Brats*, *Homer & Eddie*, *The Long Walk Home*, *Soapdish*, *Sister Act*, *The Player*, *Made in America*, *The Lion King*, *The Little Rascals*, *Corrina, Corrina*, *Star Trek: The Next Generation*, *Law and Order*, *30 Rock*, *Moonlight and Valentino*, *Ghosts of Mississippi*, *How Stella Got Her Groove Back*, *Alice in Wonderland*, *Toy Story 3*, and *Ghost*, for which she won an Oscar as Best Supporting Actress.

Along with her Academy Award, Whoopi's won Emmy nominations, Golden Globes, Tony Award, People's Choice Awards, American Comedy Awards, Kennedy Center Awards, and multiple NAACP Image Awards.

Whoopi Goldberg is a *bona fide* movie star and a cutting-edge comic who hardly rests on her many laurels. If you have any doubts, just tune in to see her weekdays as Barbara Walters' co-host on ABC-TV's *The View*.

WHERE HOLLYWOOD HIDES

WHOOPI GOLDBERG

"Normal is in the eye of the beholder."

MARTIN GORE

British Rock Icon

Songwriter and musician Martin Gore of the electronic pop band Depeche Mode has been a seminal force in the world of contemporary music for more than three decades, and he's been a Santa Barbara local for nearly as long.

Born in Essex, England, Gore caught the music bug at the age of ten, and by sixteen was lead guitarist and vocalist of the colorfully-named Norman and the Worms. His synergy with bandmates Andrew Fletcher, Vince Clarke, and David Gahan produced Depeche Mode, a collaboration that has since sold over 100 million albums and singles worldwide, and was declared "one of the greatest British pop groups of all time" by the *London Sunday Telegraph*.

When he was asked about the source of the band's name, Martin explains, "It means hurried fashion or fashion dispatch. I like the sound of that." Apparently, legions of music fans like both the name and his music, as the band's debut album *Speak & Spell* quickly rose to #10 on the British charts. Over the ensuing decade or so, the band continued to break new ground with *A Broken Frame*, *Construction Time Again*, *Some Great Reward*, *Black Celebration*, *Music for the Masses*, *Violator*, *Songs of Faith and Devotion*, *Ultra*, *Exciter*, *Playing the Angel*, and 2009's *Sounds of the Universe*.

Untold numbers of modern mega-bands were directly influenced by Depeche Mode, and trace their inspiration and lineage to Martin's writing and musicianship. "The most popular electronic band the world has ever known," as reported by *Q Magazine*, provided inspiration to such contemporary names as Pet Shop Boys, Linkin Park, Deftones, Fear Factory, Slayer, and Shakira.

Having received multiple Grammy nominations, MTV Music Awards, Echo Awards, MTV Europe Music Awards, Brit Awards, UK Music Video Awards, Q Magazine Awards, and a score of other honors, Depeche Mode and Gore himself have a secure place in the world of contemporary world music, where he has been repeatedly honored by the American Society for Composers, Authors and Publishers.

Over ten years ago, Martin discovered Santa Barbara as the perfect respite from his international fame and the media attention that accompanies such success. An admitted eBay junkie, Martin enjoys the fact that Santa Barbara allows him a certain anonymity not found in most other cities. "It's a nice town with great weather all year 'round," he says. "It leads to a very healthy lifestyle… and where else can I play soccer every weekend?"

WHERE HOLLYWOOD HIDES

Singer, actress, and entertainment industry legend, Lena Horne was front-and-center in the era that produced musical greats Duke Ellington, Billie Holiday, Ella Fitzgerald, and Sarah Vaughan.

In 1933, with her striking good looks, Lena became a Harlem Cotton Club chorus girl at the age of sixteen, and by the time she was twenty-six was one of the most highly paid entertainers in the world. Her stature as a nightclub and cabaret performer was unmatched, touring with the Charlie Barnet band, playing at the Cafe Society in New York, and recording for RCA Victor, all while appearing in early two-reel short subjects that focused on her voice and beauty.

Her nightclub notoriety brought her to the attention of MGM Studios, and she became the first African-American under contract to a major Hollywood production company. In quick succession, she appeared in *Panama Hattie*, *Cabin in the Sky*, *Ziegfeld Follies*, *Show Boat*, *Duchess of Idaho*, and *Meet Me in Las Vegas*. Always featured in those roles, of course, were Horne's impeccable vocal stylings in songs like *Stormy Weather* and *Ain't it the Truth*.

Finding herself a target of The Hollywood Blacklist for her outspoken views on politics and race, she grew disenchanted with the stand-alone nature of her roles and the studios' views about race at the time, and stepped away from her acting career. Horne didn't return to the movies again until she played in *Death of a Gunfighter* opposite Richard Widmark, another Santa Barbara resident at the time. Her subsequent appearance as Glinda in *The Wiz* and her work in MGM's *That's Entertainment* were her last major film roles.

For her musical recordings—which include thirty-five major album releases—and for her screen and television performances, as well as for her steely determination to improve the world we live in with tireless dedication to civil rights and racial equality, Lena Horne won eight Grammys, a Tony Award nomination, the New York Drama Critics Circle Award, the Drama Desk Award, an honorary doctorate from Howard University, the John F. Kennedy Center Performing Arts Award, an Emmy Award, the ASCAP Pied Piper Award, the NAACP Image Award, two Hollywood Walk of Fame stars (as recording star and as film actor), and was inducted into the International Civil Rights Walk of Fame.

After visiting friends in Montecito for the first time, Horne bought what she described as "a real storybook house" and committed fully to the laid-back Santa Barbara lifestyle. Her beauty, star power, and charisma truly made the celebrity-filled world of Santa Barbara an even better place.

LENA HORNE
"Stormy Weather"

TAB HUNTER

"Ride the Wild Surf"

If you're a frequent visitor to Santa Barbara or a local resident, you've undoubtedly bumped into Tab Hunter shopping at the local market or strolling the sands of nearby Butterfly Beach. Tab Hunter is just like the rest of us...only he happens to be a genuine Hollywood legend!

Tab was born Arthur Kelm, but at the age of fifteen used his mother's maiden name to join the U.S. Coast Guard. Discharged once his ruse was discovered, Tab returned home to follow equestrian passions at an L.A. riding academy. Soon enough, his matinee idol looks and athleticism led him to the attention of a Hollywood talent agent who promptly gave him his new name: Tab Hunter.

Before long, Tab was cast in *The Lawless*, and his magnetic screen appearance—despite the cutting of his only line of dialogue in the movie—quickly brought him a succession of other roles, including *Island of Desire*, *Battle Cry*, *The Sea Chase*, *The Burning Hills*, and *The Girl He Left Behind*.

Hunter's early career included his recording the #1 hit single *Young Love* in 1957, but his musical ambitions took a back seat to the demands of film stardom. His musical ability surfaced again in one of his most successful roles as Joe Hardy in *Damn Yankees*. He then appeared in *Lafayette Escadrille*, *They Came to Cordura*, *That Kind of Woman*, *The Pleasure of His Company*, *The Golden Arrow*, *Operation Bikini*, *Man with Two Faces*, *Ride the Wild Surf*, and *The Loved One*.

Like many of his generation, Tab found creative freedom once he was released from his studio contracts, and he gracefully transitioned to television, starring in *The Tab Hunter Show* and then being cast in more than 200 series episodes and network specials, including *Playhouse 90*, which won him an Emmy nomination.

Hunter made an elegant—if somewhat unpredictable and outrageous—appearance in *Polyester*, which was followed by memorable roles in *Grease 2*, *Lust in the Dust*, *Out of the Dark*, and *Dark Horse*.

In 2005, his autobiography *Tab Hunter Confidential: The Making of a Movie Star* became a best seller that told the candid story of a professional and personal life created by the now-extinct Hollywood studio system.

WHERE HOLLYWOOD HIDES

Even in a town known for beauty and style, this auburn-haired local native manages to stand out.

Ireland is a former "surfer girl" who began her modeling career before she even graduated from Santa Barbara's San Marcos High School. At twenty-one, she was featured in the annual *Sports Illustrated Swimsuit Issue*, eventually appearing on the cover three times, including the *25th Anniversary Swimsuit Issue*, the magazine's all-time best seller.

It didn't take long for Hollywood to notice, and Ireland was cast as Wanda in the cult classic *Alien from L.A.*, going on to appear in *Journey to the Center of the Earth*, *Side Out*, *Mr. Destiny*, *Necessary Roughness*, *Amore!*, and *Mom and Dad Save the World*.

Ireland's genuine audience appeal won her guest-starring roles in a number of TV series, including Aaron Spelling's *Melrose Place*, *Fantastic Four*, *Sabrina, the Teenage Witch*, *Suddenly Susan*, *Duckman*, *The Incredible Hulk*, *King of the Hill*, *Cosby*, *Pensacola: Wings of Gold*, and *Touched by an Angel*. Beyond her series acting work, Ireland has appeared in myriad TV specials, worked as a celebrity contestant, made multiple appearances on the late-night talk shows and daytime quiz shows, and has even acted with Kermit the Frog on *The Muppets*.

But it's beyond her screen appearances that Kathy has truly made an indelible impression on the American scene. She took an idea for a clothing line and turned it into Kathy Ireland Worldwide, a product branding and marketing enterprise with annual sales estimated at no less than $1.4 billion. Her success attracted the attention of *Forbes* magazine, who named Ireland the "prototype for model-turned-mogul."

A woman of strong beliefs and convictions, Ireland has a half-dozen books to her credit, including *Powerful Inspirations: Eight Lessons that Will Change Your Life*, *Real Solutions for Busy Moms: Your Guide to Success and Sanity*, and *Real Solutions: 52 God-Inspired Messages from My Heart*, and *Powerful Inspirations*.

As if her career didn't keep her busy enough, Kathy has always been deeply involved in her community, contributing her time and name to the March of Dimes, Feed the Children, Dream Foundation, and the Barbara Ireland Walk for the Cure.

Kathy Ireland is clearly a "hometown girl" who remains true to her origins and to her heart. All of Santa Barbara is proud to call her one of our own.

KATHY IRELAND

Homegrown Super-model

MICHAEL JACKSON

The King of Pop

Forever known as "The King of Pop," Michael Jackson came to Santa Barbara to escape the pressures of the incredible fame that was part of his daily life, and he created his personal "Neverland" on 2,700 acres of spectacular ranchland in the Santa Ynez Valley. For several years, it was one of the area's premier tourist attractions.

Jackson's career is the stuff of legend, since the day he stepped forward as lead singer of *The Jackson 5*, a "boy band" comprised of Michael and his four older brothers. At just thirteen, he broke away from the group and never looked back. As a vocalist, guitarist, pianist and percussionist, he was far more than just a pop singer. He built an unparalleled reputation as a prolific songwriter, record producer, composer, choreographer, dancer, actor, and eventually matured into a business leader, political activist, and philanthropist.

His *Thriller* remains the best-selling record album of all time, with worldwide sales beyond 110 million copies, a mark that has stood for nearly thirty years. His other albums enjoyed similar levels of phenomenal success, including *Invincible*, *HIStory: Past, Present and Future*, *Dangerous*, *Bad*, and *Off the Wall*. His lifetime record sales are estimated at 300 million...and still growing.

Michael answered the call of Hollywood, appearing in *Captain EO*, *The Wiz*, *Moonwalker*, *Michael Jackson's Ghost*, *Men in Black II*, *Miss Castaway and the Island Girls*, and *Michael Jackson's This Is It*, released just after his untimely passing.

Jackson's talents were recognized by the many honors bestowed upon him, ranging from "Artist of the Century," more than a dozen Grammys, the Grammy Lifetime Achievement Award, induction into the Grammy Hall of Fame (three times), two Hollywood Walk of Fame stars, nine different NAACP Image Awards, the Presidential Humanitarian Award, and two separate inductions into the Rock and Roll Hall of Fame. He was recognized in later life as much for his humanitarian work as for his music, receiving a Doctor of Humane Letters from Fisk University and the United Negro College Fund in 1988.

While his personal life became the subject of much controversy, Jackson rose above the swirl of sensationalism to give us musical stylings, innovative fashions, onstage versatility, and a humanitarian legacy that will continue to influence the culture for years to come.

As he himself said, "Music has been my outlet, my gift to all the lovers in this world. Through it, my music, I know I will live forever."

Having called Santa Barbara home for the past thirty years, Bruce Johnston has done more than merely live the beach lifestyle...he created the music for it!

In 1961, The Beach Boys were the vanguard of a new musical form that started right here in Southern California and quickly spread to the rest of the world. Taking the pioneering vibe of seminal artists like Dick Dale, Duane Eddy, and Link Wray...and inspired by the success of various bands from The Bel Airs to The Surfaris, The Beach Boys brought surf music into the mainstream with a groundbreaking amalgam of rock 'n' roll and doo-wop lyrics. Their first hit song, "Surfin'," paved the way for a cultural phenomenon that continues to this day.

Johnston brought his childhood training in classical music and a personal history of successful music production with him when he first joined The Beach Boys in 1965. By then, Bruce had already arranged and produced "Teenbeat," which made the charts on the *Billboard* Top Ten. That was followed in quick succession by "Take This Pearl," "Love You So"—which became a huge hit for singer Ron Holden—and "Hey Little Cobra" for The Rip Chords.

By the time Bruce was called into service by The Beach Boys, he was well-known for his production work and for his solo albums *Surfin' Round the World* and *Surfers' Pajama Party*.

In the spring of 1965 he joined The Beach Boys, replacing Glenn Campbell, who had been playing bass and singing Brian Wilson's vocal harmonies. It was a highly auspicious beginning, as Bruce's first work as a member of The Beach Boys was the everlasting hit "California Girls."

Throughout his career as "The Fifth Beach Boy," Bruce continued writing, winning a Grammy for his No. 1 *Billboard* classic "I Write the Songs," which Barry Manilow later adopted as his signature piece, and which has had worldwide sales of more than 25 million records.

Bruce Johnston, whose musical gifts to the world are timeless, is certainly the embodiment of the Santa Barbara lifestyle.

BRUCE JOHNSTON

He writes the songs...

MICHAEL KEATON

"Beatlejuice" to "Batman"

I'm...Batman!"

That single line of raspy-voiced dialogue marks one of the many highlights in the long, varied career of this Pennsylvania native who now calls a sprawling Montecito estate his personal Batcave.

The youngest of seven kids, Keaton was born with the name Michael Douglas... which he changed to avoid obvious confusion with "the other guy" of the same name. Keaton attributes his comedic instincts to his birth order, doing whatever it took as a kid to get some attention.

After two years as a speech major at Kent State, Keaton was first seen on television as one of the Flying Zucchini Brothers on *Mister Rogers' Neighborhood* in 1975. Moving to Hollywood, Keaton soon won a series of guest starring roles in the most popular television shows of the era: *All's Fair, Maude, Mary, The Tony Randall Show, The Mary Tyler Moore Show,* and *Working Stiffs*. It was while working alongside Jim Belushi in *Working Stiffs* that Keaton emerged as a quick-witted comedy performer, and was soon cast by director Ron Howard in the classic 1982 film *Night Shift* as the fast-talking "Blaze" Blazejowski.

The commercial and critical success of *Night Shift* propelled Keaton into a series of hit comedies, including *Mr. Mom, Johnny Dangerously, Gung Ho, Touch and Go, The Squeeze,* and *She's Having a Baby*.

In 1988, Keaton starred as the mischievous demon in *Beetlejuice*, directed by Tim Burton, following that with its polar opposite in *Clean and Sober*, which won Keaton the Best Actor award from the National Society of Film Critics in 1988.

Keaton was then recruited by Burton to star in one of Hollywood's biggest franchises: *Batman*. His edgy interpretation was repeated in *Batman Returns,* showcasing an intelligent wit unmatched by those who followed in the role.

Keaton next appeared in *Much Ado About Nothing* in 1993, and followed that with *My Life, The Paper, Speechless, Multiplicity,* and *Jackie Brown*. He then appeared in *Live from Baghdad*, winning a Golden Globe Best Actor nomination.

After more than forty feature films and a dozen hit TV shows, Michael Keaton remains one of Hollywood's most sought-after and nimble talents. He's got that engaging smile and a unique irreverence that makes being in the same room with him simply more fun and interesting than we have any right to expect.

WHERE HOLLYWOOD HIDES

One of Hollywood's truly "golden" girls, Cheryl Ladd has been a longtime Santa Barbara area resident, where she's just as likely to be seen on a golf course as on the red carpet.

Born Cheryl Jean Stoppelmoor and hailing from South Dakota, for the past three decades this former *Charlie's Angels* star has been the embodiment of celebrity class, grace, and glamour. At one time married to the son of silver screen icon Alan Ladd, Cheryl first came to Hollywood's attention as a singing voice of the 1970's animated television series *Josie and the Pussycats*. Once casting directors had a look at the face behind the voice, Cheryl found herself working steadily in commercials and episodic television, appearing in *The Rookies*, *The Partridge Family*, *Happy Days*, *Harry O*, *Ironside*, *The Streets of San Francisco*, and *Police Woman*...and finally landing one of the most publicized roles of all time, stepping in to replace Farrah Fawcett as Kris Munroe on *Charlie's Angels*.

By the time *Charlie's Angels* came to the end of its network run, Cheryl's fame was firmly established. Since then she has never stopped working, appearing in more than fifty television series and MOWs ranging from *Grace Kelly* to *One West Waikiki*, *Las Vegas*, and *CSI: Miami*. Her feature films include *Purple Hearts*, *Millennium*, *A Dog of Flanders* and *Walk Hard: The Dewey Cox Story*.

With such an illustrious film and television career, Cheryl's boundless energy has also seen her author a children's book, *The Adventures of Little Nettie Windship*, followed by *Token Chick: A Woman's Guide to Golfing with the Boys* (undoubtedly inspired by personal experience). As if acting and writing weren't enough, Cheryl's first love of singing is evidenced by her vocal stylings in the album *Cheryl Ladd*, which debuted on the *Billboard* charts at #38. She cut four other albums, including *Dance Forever*, *Take a Chance* and *You Make It Beautiful*; she also sang the national anthem at Super Bowl XIV, and appeared on Broadway in *Annie Get Your Gun*.

An active and tireless Santa Barbara citizen, Cheryl's philanthropy on behalf of victims of child abuse has earned her high praise and national recognition, including the Woman of the World Award from Childhelp USA. She was also the first woman to receive the Hubert H. Humphrey Humanitarian Award for her ongoing volunteerism and charitable work.

CHERYL LADD

Charlie's Angel

CHRISTOPHER LLOYD

"Back to the Future"

One of Hollywood's busiest character actors, Chris Lloyd is one of those quiet, inconspicuous Santa Barbara celebrities who is instantly recognizable wherever he's seen.

Lloyd has created some of the more memorable roles in contemporary television and film, ranging from Doc Brown in the *Back to the Future* trilogy opposite Michael J. Fox...to the unforgettable Reverend Jim of the 1970s-era ABC-TV hit *Taxi*.

Originally hailing from New England, Lloyd began his thespian career at age fourteen by apprenticing in summer stock theatrical productions. By the time he was nineteen, he was under the tutelage of master acting coach Sanford Meisner and soon appeared in a series of Broadway shows, including *Happy End*, *A Midsummer Night's Dream*, *The Seagull*, *Macbeth*, and *King Lear*.

Lloyd's theatrical film debut was as the hollow-eyed, semi-possessed character Max Taber in the Michael Douglas production *One Flew Over the Cuckoo's Nest*, alongside Jack Nicholson and Danny DeVito.

Just three years later, *Taxi* brought him widespread recognition. Over the ensuing years, he's starred in more than fifty feature films, including *The Onion Field*, *Mr. Mom*, *The Legend of the Lone Ranger*, *Star Trek III*, *Clue*, *Who Framed Roger Rabbit*, *Eight Men Out*, *DuckTales the Movie*, *Angels In the Outfield*, *The Addams Family*, *Radioland Murders*, and *My Favorite Martian*.

Lloyd has been one of those rare individuals who easily crosses over from feature films to television and back again, and is embraced by a wide range of fans. He's won three television Primetime Emmy Awards, and has received multiple Saturn Awards and Daytime Emmy Award nominations for his acting work.

When he's not fascinating us with his idiosyncratic on-screen persona, Lloyd is frequently the vocal artist behind memorable animated characters, having voiced the character of Doc Brown in *Back to the Future: The Animated Series*, as well as the character of Rasputin in 1997's *Anastasia*.

With an impressive box-office history—his starring films have grossed more than a billion dollars!—it's hardly any wonder that Christopher Lloyd continues to be among Santa Barbara's most active film stars.

Singer and megahit songwriter, Kenny Loggins may be the most active Hollywood celebrity in Santa Barbara.

A native of the Pacific Northwest, Kenny is the youngest of three boys whose musical gifts had him writing and recording original songs right out of high school. And then, just four years later, he was introduced to Jim Messina, who had already made a name for himself with the groups *Poco* and *Buffalo Springfield*.

To say that Loggins and Messina "clicked" would understate the unique harmonies that served to produce music still heard thirty-five years later on every classic rock station across the country. Their first album *Sittin' In* featured enough hit songs ("Nobody But You," "Danny's Song," "Vahevala," "House at Pooh Corner") to guarantee them a place in pop music history. Over the next four years, Loggins and Messina released five more completely original albums (*Loggins and Messina*, *Full Sail*, *On Stage*, *Mother Lode*, *So Fine*) which sold over 16 million records and established them as the 1970s' most successful duo.

Kenny's solo career took off with the release of *Celebrate Me Home* in 1976, which moved away from a folkie sound and toward the smooth, soft rock which has become his hallmark. He followed with *Nightwatch*, *Keep the Fire*, *High Adventure*, *Vox Humana*, and more than seven additional studio albums, four of which went platinum. Loggins also has credit for more than thirty hit singles, including the motion picture soundtracks for *Caddyshack*, *Footloose*, *Top Gun*, and *Over the Top*.

He continues to write and produce hits while maintaining a rigorous schedule of live performances, including occasional appearances at the Santa Barbara County Bowl.

Loggins is constantly working hard and "digging deep" as he says, and remains a tireless supporter of various local, national, and international charitable causes

Kenny Loggins' creative journey makes him a musical treasure. But it's his heart filled with music and the thrill of never-ending self-discovery that makes him a gift to the world...and a true Santa Barbara treasure.

KENNY LOGGINS

Loggins & Messina

JULIA LOUIS-DREYFUS

"Seinfeld"

After theater studies at Northwestern University where she joined a comedy troupe called The Practical Theatre Company, Julia Louis-Dreyfus was one of the youngest female cast members ever to appear on NBC's *Saturday Night Live* (at age twenty-one). She promptly moved from *SNL* to work under the direction of Woody Allen in *Hannah and Her Sisters,* and then appeared in *Troll, Soul Man,* and in *National Lampoon's Christmas Vacation* with another *SNL* alum, Chevy Chase.

But then, Larry David—who had written for *SNL* and seen her work—created Julia's career-defining role for a little show called *Seinfeld*. The character of Elaine fit Julia's persona like a glove, and the show became both a critical rave and a commercial blockbuster, running for nine remarkable seasons. *Seinfeld* saw Julia win an Emmy (and six nominations), a Golden Globe Award, multiple American Comedy Awards, and five Screen Actors Guild Awards for her portrayal as Jerry's assertive, superficial, and frequently too-honest ex-girlfriend who manages, somehow, to always get along as one of the boys.

With her place secure in the roster of television legends, she went on to a series of engaging roles as the voice of many memorable animated characters. From *Dinosaurs* to *A Bug's Life,* from *Animal Farm* to *The Simpsons,* Julia Louis-Dreyfus' vocal talents remain in constant demand.

In front of the camera, she's as active as ever, appearing in *Curb Your Enthusiasm, Watching Ellie,* and *Arrested Development.* She struck gold once again in her own hit series *The New Adventures of Old Christine,* for which she won another handful of Emmys, Golden Globe Awards, and a People's Choice Award as Favorite Female Star. She was then awarded a Hollywood Walk of Fame Star for her contributions to the broadcast television industry and was recently starring in HBO's *Veep*.

As professionally active as Julia and her husband actor–director Brad Hall are, they like nothing more than to retreat to their oceanfront Santa Barbara bungalow, which is well-known as a showcase of green design and state-of-the-art energy conservation.

They may have solid Hollywood pedigrees, but Julia Louis-Dreyfus and Brad Hall are first and foremost solid citizen-activists and the kind of neighbors who contribute mightily to the Santa Barbara we love.

Santa Barbara has long been home to this talented actor and high-energy community activist who was once named one of the "50 Most Beautiful People in the World."

But far beyond his chiseled good looks, Rob Lowe's movie and television career is an impressive body of work. With more than forty feature films to his credit and starring roles in numerous prime time TV shows, including such major hits as *The West Wing*, and *Brothers & Sisters*, Lowe has been a prominent Hollywood leading man for more than half his life.

A Virginia native, Lowe came to California as a teenager and was being cast in small roles by the time he was fourteen. At nineteen, he received his first Golden Globe nomination for Best Actor in a TV Movie, and that same year he appeared in Francis Ford Coppola's *The Outsiders*, which brought him into the young-actor-on-the-rise limelight, alongside Tom Cruise, Matt Dillon, and Diane Lane. Lowe initially gained fame as a leading member of the Brat Pack, which included rising stars Robert Downey, Jr., Demi Moore, Sean Penn, and Kevin Bacon. Lowe appeared with many of the group in *St. Elmo's Fire*, the iconic 1985 coming-of-age film in which Lowe played Billy Hicks, the ultimate frat boy.

From that point on, Lowe has always been a highly sought-after performer, appearing in *About Last Night...*, *Square Dance* (for which he was again nominated for a Golden Globe), *Masquerade*, *Wayne's World*, *Tommy Boy*, the Austin Powers trilogy, *Thank You for Smoking,* and *I Melt With You*.

Lowe's starring role in *The West Wing* won him nominations for the Screen Actors Guild Award, a Golden Globe and an Emmy, while he has appeared in more than seventy episodes of *Brothers & Sisters* as well as *Parks and Recreation, Family Guy,* and on Showtime's comedy *Californication*. He's been highly successful in the TV movie genre, appearing in *Thursday's Child, The Stand, Jane Doe, Framed, The Christmas Blessing,* and *Stir of Echoes: The Homecoming.*

As if that weren't enough, this busy actor and politically involved Santa Barbara community activist is now a twice-published author with the release of his personal memoirs, *Stories I Only Tell My Friends* and *Love Life*.

ROB LOWE

"The Brat Pack"

KARL MALDEN

"On the Waterfront"

Karl Malden, a longtime resident of Santa Barbara throughout the 1970s and 1980s, was an actor who distinguished his film sets with a true sense of gentlemanly grace. He built an unparalleled career of fifty-six feature films, an Academy Award, a Screen Actors' Guild Life Achievement Award, an Emmy, the Eugene O'Neill Theater Center Lifetime Achievement Award, a star on the Hollywood Walk of Fame, and induction into the Western Performers Hall of Fame.

Born Mladen Sekulovich, the young Chicagoan changed his name at twenty-two in order to shorten it to fit on theater marquees. Throughout his career, however, he wryly managed to interject the name "Sekulovich" into a number of films, including *Patton*, *Dead Ringer*, *Fear Strikes Out*, *Birdman of Alcatraz*, *On the Waterfront*, and even in his hit TV series *The Streets of San Francisco*.

Malden's passion for acting was gift from his father, who taught acting and produced Serbian community theatrical shows. Karl set aside college basketball dreams for a theater arts scholarship to DePaul University where he met a young actress...to whom he would be married for more than seven decades.

Malden soon made his way to New York where Elia Kazan cast him in such groundbreaking plays as Arthur Miller's *All My Sons* and Tennessee Williams' *A Streetcar Named Desire*.

Malden's transition from Broadway to Hollywood occurred when Kazan cast him (and Marlon Brando) in the film adaptation of *A Streetcar Named Desire*, for which Malden won the Oscar for Best Supporting Actor. Malden then appeared in such films as *The Sellout*, *Ruby Gentry*, *I Confess*, and *Take the High Ground*. He again supported Brando in *On the Waterfront*, with Malden again nominated as Best Supporting Actor.

From that point on, Malden's career knew no bounds, with lead roles in *Baby Doll*, *Fear Strikes Out*, *The Hanging Tree*, *One-Eyed Jacks*, *Cheyenne Autumn*, and *Nevada Smith*.

Ironically, Malden's greatest popular recognition came on the small screen when he starred in *The Streets of San Francisco* with the young Michael Douglas, after which he became the commercial spokesman for American Express, cautioning us all: "Don't leave home without it."

WHERE HOLLYWOOD HIDES

Longtime Montecito local Steve Martin continues to have an eclectic Hollywood career, having been recognized with an Emmy, three Grammys, an honorary Ph.D., a Kennedy Center Life Achievement Award, the Mark Twain Prize for American Humor, the Disney Legend Award, and the International Bluegrass Music Association's Entertainer of the Year Award.

Martin, a Texas native whose first job in show business was selling guidebooks at Disneyland, has proven to be one of the most unique writers and performers of his generation.

He dropped out of college to begin writing comedy sketches on *The Smothers Brothers Comedy Hour*, which led to his winning an Emmy at age twenty-three, and a flurry of writing gigs on *The John Denver Show*, *The Glenn Campbell Goodtime Hour*, and *The Sonny and Cher Comedy Hour*. He then had stand-up appearances on *The Tonight Show Starring Johnny Carson*, *The Gong Show*, and *Saturday Night Live*, where he has appeared as guest host no fewer than fifteen times.

It was during the 1970s that Martin released a series of sidesplitting platinum-selling comedy record albums that dominated national sales charts: *Let's Get Small*, *A Wild and Crazy Guy*, and *Comedy is Not Pretty!*

In the 1980s, Martin began to focus on his acting career, starring in *The Jerk* (which he co-wrote), *Pennies from Heaven*, *Dead Men Don't Wear Plaid*, *The Lonely Guy*, *All of Me*, *Three Amigos*, *Little Shop of Horrors*, *Roxanne*, *Dirty Rotten Scoundrels*, *Parenthood*, *My Blue Heaven*, *L.A. Story*, *Father of the Bride*, *Grand Canyon*, *HouseSitter*, *Leap of Faith*, *Father of the Bride II*, *Sgt. Bilko*, *The Out-of-Towners*, *Bowfinger*, *Cheaper by the Dozen*, *The Pink Panther*, *It's Complicated*...and *many* others.

While rising to superstar status as an actor, Martin has written numerous screenplays, books, plays, concert performances, television specials, and magazine articles, including *Picasso at the Lapin Agile*, *Underpants*, *Shopgirl*, *The Pleasure of My Company*, *Born Standing Up*, *Cruel Shoes*, *L.A. Story*, *Roxanne*, *Pure Drivel*, *Bowfinger*, and *The Alphabet from A to Y with Bonus Letter Z*.

Martin enjoys the private lifestyle of Montecito, where even the most recognizable celebrities don't draw much attention...even this "wild and crazy guy."

STEVE MARTIN

"Father of the Bride"

DENNIS MILLER

From standup to talk show icon...

Stand-up comic. Actor. Sports commentator. Political pundit. Author. Radio talk show host. Dennis Miller is the unofficial "Renaissance Man of Montecito," the acknowledged master of "the rant."

A Pittsburgh native, Miller has a genetic predisposition for acerbic, pointed wit, a trait which led to early appearances at New York's Catch A Rising Star, The Comedy Store in L.A., and *Star Search*, where (he's fond of pointing out) he came in second to the first-place winner, comedian Sinbad.

Miller's world changed in 1985 when he was drafted by *Saturday Night Live* executive producer Lorne Michaels for the role of *Weekend Update* anchor, where he created his signature line, "That's the news and I'm outta here!" That six-year stint of carefully honed insouciance rewarded him with *The Dennis Miller Show*, a series of HBO comedy specials, with a career moving across the sands of our parched entertainment landscape like the confluence of the Tigris and the Euphrates during a monsoon (as he himself might describe it).

He's authored four books, appeared as a commentator on ABC's *Monday Night Football*, and has become a fixture on the political landscape as a regular guest on Fox TV's *The O'Reilly Factor*, where he makes no excuses for his bottom-line commonsense approach to the current world scene.

Those highly rated appearances dovetail nicely with his syndicated radio talk show that draws a daily audience approaching two million listeners.

Radio's *The Dennis Miller Show*, airing nationally for three hours each weekday, has featured some of the nation's most influential movers and shakers who are willing to thrust and parry with Miller's quick wit and keen mind.

Political candidates of every persuasion are eager to engage with Miller, for his interview skills and his willingness to tell it like he sees it. Because Miller's radio show is produced in Santa Barbara, he's a local celebrity who is truly "local" each and every weekday.

WHERE HOLLYWOOD HIDES

Originally hailing from Bridgeport, Connecticut, Robert Mitchum spent many years as a true Santa Barbara local. Not many of these can claim 120 feature films to their credit; fewer can lay claim to defining an entire genre of American film. Mitchum can.

Mitchum first came to California at the age of nineteen to join his sister, who was studying acting at the Players Guild of Long Beach. Before long, with his heavy-lidded irreverence and a posture of "couldn't care less" working to his unique advantage, Mitchum was cast in a series of *Hopalong Cassidy* features, and in 1943 alone, appeared in no fewer than nineteen feature-length films, ranging from *Border Patrol* to *Minesweeper* to *Cry Havoc*.

In 1945, just nine years after he arrived in Hollywood, Mitchum was nominated as Best Supporting Actor for his role in *The Story of G.I. Joe*, and the die was cast. Mitchum's apparently effortless acting was instrumental in his becoming a *film noir* icon with the release of *When Strangers Marry* in 1944. That was soon followed by appearances in *Undercurrent, Crossfire, Out of the Past, Blood on the Moon, The Big Steal,* and *Where Danger Lives*.

Throughout his fifty-year career, Mitchum delivered a rebellious nonchalance both in character and in his personal life. Dismissive of his own talents and of filmmaking itself, his attitude was belied by powerful work in compelling films such as *The Night of the Hunter* and *Cape Fear*, where his ability to play sinister, mysterious characters was truly showcased.

Mitchum's beautiful singing voice was featured in a number of his films, including *Rachel and the Stranger* and *River of No Return*. He also recorded five albums, and even achieved "top ten" status on the country music charts with *"Little Old Wine Drinker Me."*

With changing audience tastes, Mitchum matured into contemporary classic roles in films like *Ryan's Daughter, The Friends of Eddie Coyle, The Yakuza, That Championship Season,* and the ABC miniseries *The Winds of War*.

Married for fifty-seven years, living in Santa Barbara much of that time, Mitchum left a legacy that belied his approach to life which he summed up in classic Mitchum style: *"I took what came and did the best I could with it."*

ROBERT MITCHUM

"I never changed anything except my socks and my underwear."

PETER NOONE

"I'm Henry the Eighth, I am…"

With a career that got a running start at the age of fifteen, Peter Noone, the ever young, always ebullient, and perpetually appealing lead singer of Herman's Hermits, has been a Santa Barbara local for more than twenty years.

A native of Lancashire, England, Peter Noone possesses longevity as a singer that is no accident, having started his career by winning the Outstanding Young Musician Award while at St. Bede's College and Manchester School of Music.

When Noone—the youngest of the Hermits, who was already an experienced British soap opera actor—formed a "beat" band, the band's clean, up-tempo harmonies touched a nerve in music fans worldwide. Their youthful energy and appeal helped to quickly drive their first hit, "I'm Into Something Good," to the top of both British and American charts. That smash was quickly followed by "Mrs. Brown, You've Got a Lovely Daughter," "Can't You Hear My Heartbeat," and the comedic "I'm Henry the Eighth, I Am" (in which Noone took his English accent to a regional extreme).

Noone and the Hermits appeared in a number of feature films of the 1960s, including *Pop Gear*, *When the Boys Meet the Girls*, *Hold On!*, and *Mrs. Brown, You've Got a Lovely Daughter*. As their pop status challenged that of the Beatles, Noone carried lead vocals for more classic pop tunes, including "Dandy," and "There's a Kind of Hush." The boys put out five studio albums in a period of three years: *Herman's Hermits*, *Both Sides of Herman's Hermits*, *There's a Kind of Hush All Over The World*, *Blaze*, and *Mrs. Brown, You've Got a Lovely Daughter*.

As pop music evolved, Noone struck out as a solo performer, building a remarkable career beyond recording. Noone has appeared on Broadway in *The Pirates of Penzance*, has hosted numerous music and awards shows, was named "VH1's Sexiest Artist" in 2001, and continues to make surprise guest appearances on TV, the most recent of which was on *American Idol*.

Even with such a glorious past, Noone is not exactly resting on his laurels. His tour schedule remains packed, and he truly lives the traveling minstrel life, jetting across the world to bring his music and his indefatigable energy and cheer to endless legions of fans.

Very few Hollywood celebrities can match the impact that this six-foot six-inch Texas farmboy-turned-actor has had on Santa Barbara.

Fess Parker's life was an eighty-five-year-long journey that took him from Fort Worth, Texas, to World War II's South Pacific battlefront, back to his home state for a degree in theater arts, to Hollywood for an amazing career as a television and film star, and finally to Santa Barbara where he transformed the city's waterfront from a "hobo jungle" to a sparkling tourist destination that continues to attract millions of visitors and locals every year.

After his wartime service, Parker started his show business career as an extra, standing around in the background of scenes in Broadway's *Mister Roberts*, with Henry Fonda in the lead. That quickly led to a small role in *Untamed Frontier* and a Warner Bros. Studios contract that put him in a series of westerns and war movies like *Springfield Rifle*, *Island in the Sky*, *The Bounty Hunter*, and *Battle Cry*.

It wasn't long before he was discovered by Walt Disney, who cast him as the title character in *Davy Crockett*, a short-lived television series that soon had every kid in the country wearing a coonskin cap and longing for a buckskin jacket. Disney quickly put him under a contract that soon had him bringing his oversized persona to movies like *The Great Locomotive Chase*, *Westward Ho, the Wagons!*, *Old Yeller*, and *The Light in the Forest*. Parker easily made the crossover between feature films and television, and continued to appear on the small screen in shows like *Annie Oakley* and *Mr. Smith Goes to Washington*.

Once free of his Disney contract, Parker's star soared with *Daniel Boone*, an ABC series that stood at the top of television ratings for six years and saw him producing, directing, and leveraging his fame into a wide variety of business enterprises...one of which was land development.

In the 1970s, Parker began his real estate career modestly enough, building a handful of upscale mobile home parks. Twenty years later his vision for a major resort complex on Santa Barbara's undeveloped waterfront became a reality. Today, *Fess Parker's Doubletree Resort* remains a powerful magnet for tourists, locals, and conventioneers.

Parker retired to Santa Ynez in the 1990s, where he created the Fess Parker Winery, another landmark of this genuine Santa Barbara–Hollywood Celebrity.

FESS PARKER

From "Davy Crockett" to Santa Barbara trailblazer

KATY
PERRY

Little did anyone know that when Katheryn Elizabeth Hudson was born at Santa Barbara Cottage Hospital, she would become internationally famous as Katy Perry.

Katy's musical talent was obvious even at the age of nine when she began singing in church. While her early exposure to musical genres was strictly limited to Christian gospel, it was a teen slumber party that first introduced her to the pop world of Alanis Morissette and Freddie Mercury. By the time she was fifteen, she'd already been noticed by Nashville producers who helped make her first "gospel rock" recording...an effort that met with little commercial success.

Surviving early disappointments in a fickle recording industry, Katy eventually wound up at Capitol Records where her songwriting was given vigorous support. It was at Capitol that her persona as a larger-than-life, vivaciously coquettish tongue-in-cheek pop star was honed. Her first release for the label, "Ur So Gay," gained her initial recognition if only for the controversial subject matter it referenced. Her second release, "I Kissed a Girl," became a major breakthrough hit and drove the sales of her 2008 album *One of the Boys* to the top of the charts.

Katy's next album, *Teenage Dream*, sold over two million copies just in the U.S., with its lead single "California Gurls" hitting the *Billboard* magazine charts for more than six weeks. Subsequent releases, including her collaboration with Kanye West on the single "E.T.," have only guaranteed her position as one of the most successful female pop stars of all time. She's the first female to ever produce five #1 *Billboard* Hot 100 songs in one album, a record matched only by Michael Jackson.

Katy has made multiple film and television appearances on shows like *The Young and the Restless, American Idol, Sesame Street, The X Factor, Saturday Night Live, How I Met Your Mother,* and even *Extreme Makeover: Home Edition*. In 2012 she produced and starred in *Katy Perry: Part of Me*, which has now become the fourth-highest-grossing music concert film of all time.

Most endearing to her Santa Barbara followers, Katy remains true to herself and to her roots. More than once she's made surprise appearances at local Santa Barbara clubs and has even dropped in at her local alma mater, Dos Pueblos High School. She may be one of the world's biggest pop stars, but she'll always be our "California Gurl."

Take a drive up U.S.101. Stop for gas anywhere from State Street north to Gaviota...and the guy pumping his own gas next to you just might be one of the most popular screen stars of his generation...because you're smack dab in the middle of Brad Pitt territory.

When Brad and Angelina Jolie aren't jetting between their New Orleans home and the Santa Barbara International Film Festival...they just might be hanging out at their sprawling Santa Barbara oceanfront property right down the hill from the late President Reagan's Rancho del Cielo.

Born in Oklahoma and raised in Springfield, Missouri, Pitt went from Kickapoo High to the University of Missouri where performed in school plays and fraternity shows. But with an abiding interest in films—"a portal into different worlds for me"—he took a flyer and went to Los Angeles to take acting lessons and work in a series of menial jobs.

Pitt's boyish looks and aw-shucks charm soon won him small parts in television soap operas and sitcoms, including *Another World* for NBC-TV and ABC's *Growing Pains*. Those were soon followed by appearances on CBS' *Dallas*, *21 Jump Street*, *Head of the Class*, *Freddy's Nightmares*, and *Thirtysomething*.

Pitt's true breakout came in the role of J.D, in 1991's *Thelma & Louise*. That small part propelled him to a career that has seen him starring in *A River Runs Through It*, *Kalifornia*, *Interview with the Vampire*, *Legends of the Fall*, *Se7en*, *12 Monkeys*, *Seven Years in Tibet*, *Meet Joe Black*, *Fight Club*, *Snatch*, *The Mexican*, *Spy Game*, *Ocean's Eleven*, *Troy*, and *Mr. & Mrs. Smith*.

Pitt has twice been named "America's Sexiest Man Alive" by *People* magazine, and has won multiple awards and nominations across the board for his acting and producing endeavors. He's been recognized with MTV Movie Awards, Golden Globes, BAFTA Awards, Academy Award nominations, and a handful of Film Critics Awards. Just within the past few years he's starred in and produced such memorable films as *The Departed*, *The Curious Case of Benjamin Button*, *The Tree of Life*, *Moneyball*, *World War Z*, *Fury*, and *Twelve Years a Slave*, for which he won an Oscar.

With a personal and professional life that has been the focus of worldwide attention for more than a decade, there aren't many stars in the universe that shine as brightly as Brad Pitt...and Santa Barbara remains the perfect place for him to unwind and step out of that media glare, for our little red-tiled town is truly "where Hollywood hides."

BRAD PITT

"I'm just a grown man who puts on makeup."

RONALD REAGAN

From the Silver Screen to The Oval Office

As the only genuine Hollywood celebrity to ever hold office as President of the United States of America, there may never have been a more prominent citizen of Santa Barbara than Ronald Reagan.

Reagan's life story is legendary: born the grandson of Irish immigrants in Tampico, Illinois, "Dutch" played football and captained the swim team at Eureka College before he broke into radio broadcasting, reading wire reports of baseball games.

A 1937 trip to California provided Reagan the chance to take a screen test at Warner Bros. Studios, and he soon found himself under contract as an actor. Within just a few years he had appeared in nearly twenty movies, including *Dark Victory* with Bette Davis, *Knute Rockne, All American*, and *Santa Fe Trail* with Errol Flynn. Other classics of the period included *Kings Row*, *Hell's Kitchen*, and *Bedtime for Bonzo*.

After World War II, Reagan became active in union politics and was eventually elected president of the fractious Screen Actors Guild, while he embraced the new medium of television as the host of *General Electric Theater*.

Reagan found himself drawn to conservative issues and eventually winning the support of the Republican Party. With a gift for phrasing, it was Reagan's famous "A Time for Choosing" speech in support of Barry Goldwater in 1964 that truly propelled him to the forefront of political up-and-comers. Just two years later, Reagan was nominated for governor of California, an office he subsequently held for two full terms.

His profile within national politics grew, and after a failed bid for the presidential nomination in 1976, he ultimately defeated incumbent Jimmy Carter in the 1980 presidential campaign. Reagan was re-elected in 1984 at age sixty-nine, the oldest man ever elected to the White House.

As Reagan's second presidential term came to a close, he and his wife Nancy began spending more and more time in Santa Barbara, frequently vacationing at Rancho del Cielo, their 688-acre spread just north of the city. Known as "The Western White House," the humble ranch is emblematic of the simple tastes and down-home midwestern roots of the man who was truly the most famous of all Santa Barbara's citizens.

Along time Santa Barbara local, Alan Thicke has certainly come a long way from his roots. This high school homecoming king originally from Ontario, Canada, found his show business calling early in life.

Getting his start as a writer—at the age of nineteen—on *The Tommy Hunter Show*, the longest-running country music show in North America, his never-ending writing credits include work on *Time for Living, That's Show Biz, The Paul Lynde Show, The Bobby Darin Show, The Flip Wilson Special, Don Adam's Screen Test, A Special Olivia Newton-John, The Barry Manilow Special, The Richard Pryor Show, Fernwood Tonight,* and his own 1980s talk show *Thicke of the Night*.

As if the life of a full-time writer wasn't enough, Thicke has also become a fixture on television ever since his acting debut at age twenty-two on *It's Our Stuff*. He's appeared in a wide range of series, from *Time for Living* and *Perry Mason* to multiple performances on *The Love Boat*, and a long list of TV movies including *Not Quite Human, Hitting Home, The Great American Sex Scandal,* and 2013's *Bad Management* for ABC Television.

While being eminently "castable" for a wide range of both dramatic and comedic roles, Thicke's irreverent and intelligent wit has made him a fixture as a popular emcee, keynote speaker, Las Vegas headliner, and game show host. His energy and charm have made rating successes out of shows like *The Emmy Awards, Pictionary, ABC's Disney Christmas,* multiple Miss USA and Miss Universe pageants, *ABC's Animal Crack-Ups,* and CNBC's *Today's Man*.

Uniquely multi-talented, Thicke has also had a complete career as a composer, having created the theme songs for major hit TV shows like *Wheel of Fortune, The Joker's Wild, Celebrity Sweepstakes, The Wizard of Odds, The Facts of Life,* and *Diff'rent Strokes*.

Even with multiple Emmys to his name, what truly made Alan Thicke instantly recognizable on any street in America was his long-running role as Jason Seaver, the stay-at-home dad doing his best to raise a family in *Growing Pains*. The show was a major television series milestone and firmly established Thicke as a positive parenting role model. With that platform, he's authored *How Men Have Babies: The Pregnant Father's Survival Guide,* and *How To Raise Kids Who Don't Hate You*.

His new light-hearted reality show, *The Thicke of Things,* features his life with his three sons...and only further establishes Alan Thicke as a true local enjoying the ultimate dream of living and working right here in Santa Barbara.

ALAN THICKE

Man of Many Talents

JOHN TRAVOLTA

"Saturday Night Fever" Superstar

With a nonstop career spanning four decades, few in Hollywood can match the talents of this genuine Jersey boy. Born the youngest of six kids, by the age of seventeen John Travolta knew exactly what he wanted to do...and he began doing it.

Dropping out of high school, in 1971 Travolta left New Jersey, made his way to Broadway, and won a supporting role in the touring company of *Grease*, a show that would later deliver lasting fame to the young actor-singer-dancer. He followed that with another song-and-dance role in *Over Here!* on Broadway, which encouraged him to head for Hollywood.

It was at Universal City Studios where he first got before the cameras with an early bit part on NBC-TV's *Emergency!* More work followed quickly, and Travolta appeared in Brian De Palma's *Carrie* just before he won the role of Vinnie Barbarino in the ABC-TV smash hit *Welcome Back, Kotter*. In the second year of production on that show, Travolta recorded "Let Her In," a hit single that made it to the top of the *Billboard* charts, and while still working on *Kotter*, he was cast as Tony Manero in *Saturday Night Fever*, the movie that catapulted him to international stardom and won him an Academy Award nomination.

The following year, he played the lead opposite Olivia Newton-John in *Grease*, and soon after appeared in *Urban Cowboy*, the hit film that inspired a generation's love of country music.

Comedy roles followed with *Look Who's Talking*, *Look Who's Talking Too*, and *Look Who's Talking Now*. Then, in an abrupt character turn, Travolta appeared in *Pulp Fiction* as hit man Vincent Vega, winning another Academy Award nomination. Travolta followed that with the films *Get Shorty*, *Face Off*, *A Civil Action*, *Primary Colors*, *The General's Daughter*, *Wild Hogs*, *Hairspray*...and dozens more. With over fifty feature films, ten record albums, and more than two dozen singles to his credit, Travolta is one of the few who has made the transition from television to motion picture stardom.

An erstwhile Santa Barbara resident, Travolta has been a frequent visitor to town, often landing at the local airport in one of the several jets he personally pilots.

An ebullient entertainer and audience favorite, Travolta was recently presented with the Santa Barbara International Film Festival's Kirk Douglas Award for Excellence in Film, by Kirk Douglas himself.

There may be no other celebrity on the planet—and certainly none other in Santa Barbara—who more completely exemplifies the "Where Hollywood Hides" escape from the pressures of show business to live a quiet, off-the-red-carpet lifestyle than Montecito resident Oprah Winfrey.

Raised with a singular work ethic and the self-discipline to match, Oprah graduated from Tennessee State with a degree in communications, and the Miss Black Tennessee crown. Her education, her verve, and her determination soon had her appearing as a news anchor and quiz show host on Nashville television.

When Oprah appeared on Chicago's *AM Chicago* morning show, she pulled the show's ratings out of the cellar and took it to #1 in its timeslot. Within two years she was hosting *The Oprah Winfrey Show*. Expanding to a national audience, she eventually replaced Phil Donahue as America's daytime talk show leader.

After negotiating ownership of her syndicated show, Oprah quickly branched out to produce and star in her own prime time miniseries, *The Women of Brewster Place*, which followed her Academy Award nomination for Best Supporting Actress in Steven Spielberg's *The Color Purple*. Oprah's production company, Harpo Films, has produced quality programming that reflects her serious artistic sensibilities, including *Beloved* and *Their Eyes Were Watching God*. With the unveiling of Oxygen Media, the publication of *O, The Oprah Magazine*, and ownership of the internationally syndicated *Oprah Winfrey Show,* this Montecito resident is now among the world's wealthiest women.

An active supporter of children's rights around the globe, she has donated both her time and her money to foster the cause of education throughout Africa. The recent tally of her philanthropy approaches the $500 million mark and has earned her numerous accolades, including being the 2002 Emmy recipient of the first Bob Hope Humanitarian Award. Oprah has been described by many as the world's most powerful woman, and as "one of the 100 people who most influenced the 20th Century."

Oprah Winfrey is truly one of a kind, and certainly one of our most inspirational Santa Barbara neighbors.

OPRAH WINFREY

"Dwell in possibility."

JONATHAN WINTERS

Santa Barbara's Funnyman

Actor. Comedian. Artist. Author. Jonathan Winters, for many years a Santa Barbara fixture, was one of the most inventive and creative minds of his generation.

Born in Dayton, Ohio, Winters left home at seventeen, joined the Marine Corps, and served more than two years in the Pacific before returning home to enter a talent contest with the hope of winning a new wristwatch. He won the watch and discovered his true calling: making people laugh.

That early success led to a job in local radio where he discovered his uncanny talent for characters and ad-libbing. After a short stint on WBNS-TV in Columbus, Ohio, he set off for New York and was soon booked as a stand-up comic in a handful of nightclubs. His growing reputation as a completely unpredictable talent got him recruited as a semi-regular on the CBS Sunday morning show *Omnibus*, where he quickly came to national attention.

Over a career spanning more than fifty years, Winters appeared on every TV variety show imaginable, including *The Gary Moore Show, Arthur Godfrey's Talent Scouts, The Jack Paar Show, The Steve Allen Show, The Tonight Show, The Jonathan Winters Show, The Wacky World of Jonathan Winters, Hee Haw, Rowan & Martin's Laugh-In,* and *The Carol Burnett Show*...not to mention innumerable quiz shows, sitcoms, and talk shows.

Winters' television credits are nearly matched by his amazing track record in movies, including *It's a Mad, Mad, Mad, Mad World, Oh Dad, Poor Dad, The Loved One, The Russians Are Coming, The Russians Are Coming, Viva Max, The Fish That Saved Pittsburgh,* and *Moon Over Parador*...and the account of his voiceover work in both live action and animated feature films could fill this entire book.

While building this unparalleled film and television history, Winters recorded his routines and zany characters on no fewer than two dozen comedy albums, generating ten Grammy nominations. He was the recipient of numerous other awards, including the American Comedy Award, a Golden Globe nomination as Best Actor, a Golden Laurel Award, an Emmy Award, the Kennedy Center Mark Twain Prize for American Humor, and a star on the Hollywood Walk of Fame.

Jonathan Winters never shied away from his fans. If he saw you in line at the local bank and you laughed at his jokes, then he made you a friend for life...and the next time he saw you, he knew you by name.

We certainly won't forget his.

Of all the spectacular, celebrity-driven events taking place throughout the city in any given year—from monster charity balls and fundraising events to professional polo tournaments and yacht races—none has the glamour or celebrity cachet of the Santa Barbara International Film Festival.

Originally established in 1985 as a nonprofit showcase for independent American and international films, the festival was initially funded by private donations, making its way through a series of leadership challenges as genuine Hollywood recognition and credibility came slowly.

With the arrival of current executive director Roger Durling—a lifelong devotee of all things cinema, a prolific writer, and a local cafe owner—things began to change. Moving the festival dates to the weeks leading up to the Academy Awards and bringing his charismatic, accessible persona into the mix, Durling brought passion, identity, direction, and an entrepreneurial spirit that has put the SBIFF front-and-center among the most prestigious and celebrity-filled festivals on the planet.

Operating with the support of corporate sponsors, the festival celebrates filmmakers from around the world as well as fledgling local movie talents, and has become an annual magnet for all of Hollywood.

Now scheduled each year between the Sundance Film Festival and Hollywood's Academy Awards, Roger Durling's impeccably managed event has become known as "The Oscars Festival." The proof of the SBIFF's importance to the film community is apparent with recent appearances at local venues by Robert Redford, Emma Thompson, Jared Leto, Jennifer Lawrence, Quentin Tarantino, Helen Mirren, James Cameron, Clint Eastwood, Leonardo DiCaprio, Kate Winslet, Viola Davis, Martin Scorsese, Robert De Niro, Ben Affleck, Kirk Douglas, Amy Adams, Colin Firth, Bruce Dern and...the list goes on.

It's an impressive record of Academy Award winners that contribute to the Santa Barbara International Film Festival's reputation as a must-stop appearance for serious Oscar hopefuls...and as the ultimate tourist event of the year.

WHERE HOLLYWOOD HIDES

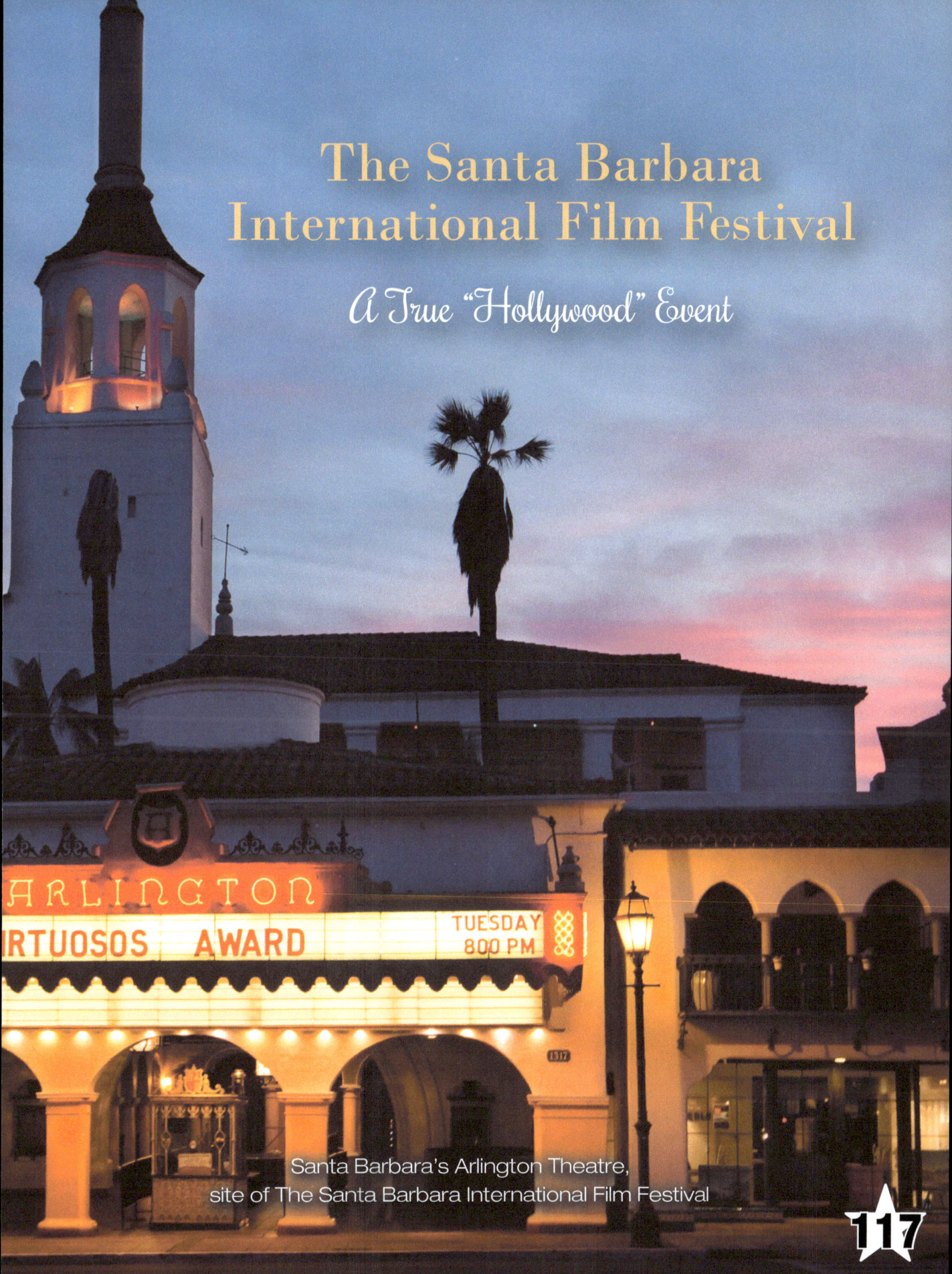

ROGER DURLING

Director of The Santa Barbara International Film Festival

One of the great attractions of the SBIFF is the series of tributes and awards presented throughout the ten days of the festival to stars like these…

Bruce Dern
2014 Modern Master Award

Oprah Winfrey
2014 Montecito Award

Robert Redford
2014 Virtuoso Award

Cate Blanchett
2014 Outstanding Performance for Blue Jasmine

Jennifer Lawrence
2013 Outstanding Performance for Silver Linings Playbook

Viola Davis
2011 Outstanding Performance for The Help

James Franco
2010 Outstanding Performance for 127 Hours

Colin Firth
2009 Outstanding Performance for A Single Man

Penélope Cruz
2008 Outstanding Performance for Elegy

Angelina Jolie
2007 Outstanding Performance for A Mighty Heart

Helen Mirren
2006 Outstanding Performance for The Queeen

Heath Ledger
2005 Outstanding Performance for Brokeback Mountain

Kate Winslett
2004 Outstanding Performance for Eternal Sunshine of the Spotless Mind

Charlize Theron
2003 Outstanding Performance for Monster

WHERE HOLLYWOOD HIDES

Recent Santa Barbara Productions

Santa Barbara has long been a part of the "Hollywood scene"...and with the SBIFF heading into another year and screening nearly two dozen world premieres from more than 40 countries, that will never change...for this is truly "where Hollywood hides".

Flying A Studios director Frank Borzage
calling the shots on "Land O' Lizards", c. 1916

Courtesy Santa Barbara Historical Museum

Since the days of The Flying A Studios, Santa Barbara has been a magnet for Hollywood. In just the past decade "The Mission City" has attracted a wide range of motion picture and television productions, including—

2012 The Bet
2012 Montecito Ballroom
2012 Mucho Dinero
2012 Say Yes to the Dress
2012 Falling Skies
2012 Ready for Love
2012 I Love Jennie
2012 Ready for Love
2012 Who You Think You Are
2012 Perfect Present
2012 Married to the Game
2012 Hollywood Exes
2011 The Real L Word
2011 Uncorked
2011 Christmas Wedding Tail
2011 Top Gear
2011 Little People Big World
2011 Man Vs. Food Nation
2011 DC Cupcakes
2011 X Factor
2011 Extreme Makeover
2011 The Amazing Race
2010 Real Housewives of Beverly Hills
2010 No Strings Attached
2010 Hoods
2010 Undercovers
2010 Rites of Passage
2009 Uncorked
2009 It's Complicated

2009 Bad Girls
2009 Nitro Circus
2009 The Othersiders
2009 Inside Luxury Travel
2009 More to Love
2009 Back in Wedding Shape
2009 You're Hired
2009 Kathy Griffin
2009 Somewhere
2009 Flying Lessons
2009 Ghost Adventures
2009 Love Life
2008 Rachael's Vacation
2008 Momma's Boys
2008 Samantha Brown
2008 Generation Gap
2008 A Place in the Sun
2008 A View From Here
2008 Psych
2007 Jolene
2007 American Son
2007 Ten Years Later
2007 Annabel Lee
2007 The Dog Whisperer
2007 Hell's Kitchen
2007 The Real OC
2006 Life On the D List
2006 The Perfect Day
2006 Grind House

2006 Pirates of the Caribbean
2006 Alpha Dog
2006 Mickey Fish
2006 Let's Go to Prison
2006 There Will Be Blood
2006 The Bachelor
2006 Top Chef 2
2006 California Connected
2006 Trading Spaces
2006 The Messengers
2006 Ex-Wives Club
2006 Death Ride
2005 Monk
2005 Best In Town
2005 Curb Your Enthusiasm
2005 iCandy
2005 The Wrath 2005 Oprah Winfrey Show
2005 JAG
2004 Flight of the Phoenix
2004 Monster-In-Law
2003 Hidalgo
2003 Seabiscuit
2003 The Bachelor
2003 Spartan

WHERE HOLLYWOOD HIDES

Photo Credits

Santa Barbara Historical Museum

pp. ii, iv, 4, 5, 62, 63, 120, 122, 123

Shutterstock.com

Alec Michael	p. 119
Byron Purvis/AdMedia	p. 119
carrie-nelson	pp. 11, 73, 119
Helga Esteb	pp. 36, 40, 70, 81, 102, 119
holbox	pp. 7, 9
Jaguar PS	p. 119
Joe Seer	p. 119
Michael Germana	p. 119
Paul Smith/Feature Flash	pp. 19, 28, 31, 39, 44, 56, 60, 65, 78, 105, 110, 113, 119
Randy Miramontez	p. 98
S_bukley	pp. 35, 48, 55, 59, 82, 86, 89, 94, 119
Scott Kirkland	p. 119
Cinemafestival/Shutterstock	Back cover

ImageCollect.com

Byron Purvis/AdMedia	p. 118
D. Long/Globe Photos Inc.	p. 32
Dan Harr/AdMedia	p. 93
Donald Sanders/AdMedia	p. 12
Globe Photos Inc.	pp. 15, 97, 98
Graham Witby Boot/Globe Photos Inc.	p. 16
Jonathan Alcorn/ZUMA Press/Globe Photos Inc.	p. 101
Lisa Rose/Globe Photos Inc.	p. 27
Mark Allan/alpha/Globe Photos Inc.	p. 20
Mark Reinstein/ipol/Globe Photos Inc.	p. 106
Nancy Kaszerman/ZUMA Press	p. 47
Nate Cutler/Globe Photos Inc.	p. 90
Paula Colella/Michelson/Globe Photos Inc.	p. 114
Phil Roach/ipol/Globe Photos Inc.	p. 51
Rangefinders/Globe Photos Inc.	pp. 44, 106
Rick Mackler/Rangefinders/Globe Photos Inc.	p. 23
S_bukley/Globe Photos Inc.	pp. 43, 109
Smp/Globe Photos Inc.	p. 110
Uppa/ipol/Globe Photos Inc.	p. 24

Alamy.com

Interfoto/Alamy	p. 8
Keystone Pictures USA/Alamy	p. 1
Scott London/Alamy	p. 117
United Archives/GmbH/Alamy	p. 52

Butterfly Beach Media LLC

R.L. McCullough pp. i, 2, 3, 13, 24, cover

WHERE HOLLYWOOD HIDES

On location "out West" in Santa Barbara
with the Flying A cast & crew, c. 1917

Courtesy Santa Barbara Historical Museum

WHERE HOLLYWOOD HIDES

About the Authors

Bob McCullough and Suzanne Herrera first met at Universal City Studios as they were beginning their show business careers.

"Almost-almost famous"

By the time they said their wedding vows within a stone's throw of the studio back lot, Suzanne was appearing in TV shows like *Emergency, Quincy, Falcon Crest, Helter Skelter, High Tide, Kojak, The Rockford Files, The Incredible Hulk, Battlestar Galactica, International Airport* and *Fantasy Island* and was one of the commercial voices on The Wolfman Jack Radio Show. When asked about her acting career, Suzanne jokingly refers to herself as "almost-almost famous." She's written for *Falcon Crest* and *Zorro*, and continues to develop feature film and book projects.

"Dr Bob"

Bob has produced, directed, and written mini-series, movies, and weekly shows ranging from *Hollywood Wives* and *Falcon Crest* to *JAG, Baywatch, High Tide, Ohara, Six Million Dollar Man*, and *Star Trek: The Next Generation*. He is often sought after as "Dr. Bob," for his ability to bring life to ailing screenplays.

Bob and Suzanne live in Santa Barbara and count among their friends numerous entertainment industry notables. You can hear their engaging conversational podcast—devoted to the classic years of movies, television and music—on iTunes and at www.WhereHollywoodHides.com.

Butterfly Beach Media LLC
1187 Coast Village Rd., ste. 512
Santa Barbara, Calif. 93108
www.ButterflyBeachMedia.com

www.ingramcontent.com/pod-product-compliance
Lightning Source LLC
Chambersburg PA
CBHW040738150426
42811CB00064B/1785